Without Controversy

Over 20 Bible Controversies
Answered

Pastor Rick Strawcutter

 Liberty Press

Without Controversy
Over 20 Bible Controversies Answered
By Pastor Rick Strawcutter

Published by:
Liberty Press
Post Office Box 339
Adrian, Michigan Occupation Zone 49221

Orders@Proclaimliberty.com

Unattributed quotations are by Rick Strawcutter.

ISBN, print ed.   0-9719119-0-8

First printing 2002

Acknowledgements

This book would not be possible without the help of an incredible number of people. Hundreds of friends, teachers, mentors, fellow laborers with Christ and just plain folks, have all contributed to the sum total of what you will read in these pages.

Brenda Herr was invaluable as an editor. Paul Slusser is solely responsible for the cover design and concept. What a guy!

Many people supplied critical analysis and warnings, some of which I listened to, some of which I ignored.

My gracious wife Betty is to be applauded for simply being willing to be my life's partner and take the heat that accompanies "guilt by association." I guess I should say at this point that the views expressed within these pages are mine alone, and do not necessarily reflect those of my immediate family members and other people that I love and owe so much to.

God only knows where my lost soul might have ended up without Pastor Douglas Stephens having the vision and courage to come to Grand Ledge Michigan in 1963 and there founding a United Pentecostal Church that ultimately would become my spiritual birth place. He has always loved and stood by me as a great pastor and friend. However, he, along with a number of my other ministerial friends, do not concur with all of my doctrinal or political views. Regardless, their love and respect for me speaks volumes of their Christian charity, for which I am so grateful.

Truly, when I consider my asset portfolio, my friends are at the top of the list. Without people to interact God's love with, where would any of us be? The members of "The Church" on Bent Oak Highway are the greatest people of all. I love them each and every one! Thanks for letting me be your Pastor.

Contents

About The Author

Pastor Rick Strawcutter started out life in 1950. He graduated from Michigan's Grand Ledge High School in 1968, where he boxed Golden Gloves, was voted "most original" by his class and founded the UFO Club. He is distinguished as a college drop-out of Indiana University, with one additional year of law school to his credit and a pilot's license. His favorite educational quote is the one given by Mark Twain when he was asked about the extent of his education. "The extent of my education has been the entirety of my life, except for those years I was in public school."

He married a beautiful, intelligent and highly talented lady from Albion Michigan named Betty. She is an elementary teacher. Together they produced two outstanding kids William and Faith.

In 1971 he was the youngest single direct distributor in Amway Corporation. By 1976 he was married, thoroughly saved and ready to become the Pastor of the fantastic church he currently leads in Adrian Michigan.

Pastor's first publishing experience was a text on economics and politics called "Bankers, Lawyers and Judges - The Unholy Trinity. In 1996 he founded one of the longest running, so-called pirate radio stations in U.S. history called Radio Free Lenawee at 99.3 fm. He is a recognized expert on radar traffic defenses.

A passionate lover of freedom and liberty, he has produced and distributed politically incorrect video tapes all over the world and has made appearances on the "Phil Donahue Show" and countless other radio talk shows. His congregation reflects his zest for living. He calls them the greatest people this side of heaven. When asked how great are they? He just replies, "Come and see for yourself. They're so great, you wouldn't believe me if I told you."

Warning!

There is one matter I feel I should warn you of. Your author recently has admitted that he has a "thinking" problem. It is something like a "drinking" problem.

I come from a family of "non-thinkers." No one I knew was a "thinker." So, I really shouldn't have had any natural tendencies or inherited weaknesses in this area, but nonetheless it happened to me. It could happen to you, or someone you love, too.

It all started when someone I long suspected of being a "thinker," offered me a "social think." I declined, explaining that I was a "non-thinker," but they were insistent that I try just one "think."

I hesitated, but, I figured what could one little "think" hurt. That was my first mistake. That first "think." I really liked the feeling it gave me. So, I had another "think" and before I realized what was happening, I was taking one "think" after another.

It's embarrassing to admit it now, but I really got carried away with myself and before the night was over, I was pretty well "thunk."

What would my friends and family say? Rick Strawcutter, a problem "thinker." I did my best to keep it hidden, but when you have a "thinking" problem its hard to hide. Word gets around.

Besides the "social thinking" that was so easy to do, I found myself sneaking off to have a "think," all on my own. At other times, I would seek out places where "thinkers" would congregate so I could hang-out with other "thinkers."

When you surround yourself with "thinkers" everything seems so normal. But sooner or later you have no choice but to return to

1

the world of "non-thinkers."

In that world, you're forced to lead a kind of double life. You do your best to talk and act like a "non-thinker" But try as I would, it was useless, "non-thinkers" can tell a "thinker" a mile off.

It wasn't long until my "thinking" began to affect my employment. I was getting caught "thinking" on the job. People notice when you "think." "Thinking" can interfere with just about everything.

Finally my closest friends and family surrounded me one night and told me, "Look Rick, we care about you and we want to help you with your problem."

"What problem, what are you talking about?" (I was in denial) But they had me outnumbered.

"Your "thinking" problem is out of control" they insisted, "you've got to stop this constant "thinking!"

They were right. I thought I could control it, but in no time at all I had become a "heavy thinker!"

I later realized it wasn't me that they were so concerned about. It was themselves. When "non-thinkers" are around even one single "thinker," the "non-thinker's" life can be a veritable hell of mental confusion. A "non-thinkers" life is very simple and uncluttered and they like to keep it that way. I know, I was a "non-thinker" for years.   Until that first "social think....."

I tried all the traditional cures. I tried watching television and forced myself to laugh at the sitcoms and stupid jokes that "non-thinkers" enjoy to no end, but it only drove me to more temptations to "think."

I went so far as to join "thinkers anonymous" for a while, but I just couldn't bring myself to stand up in front of that crowd of pitiful people and confess that,

"My name is Rick Strawcutter and I have a thinking Problem." How humiliating!

I even immersed myself in sports and meaningless chatter with "non-thinkers" about the latest fads, the weather and movie stars. I pretended to be enriched by the drivel which filled the daily newspapers. But it was hopeless. After a relatively short time of "non-thinking," I would find myself over-come with an insatiable desire to have a "think." Any "think." Just lead me to the nearest "think." A lite "think." A mixed "think" it didn't matter. I just had to have a "think."

Sometimes I'd stay "thunk" for days. Nobody could stand me. Except for my "thinking" friends. They understood. They all had the same problem with their "non-thinking" friends.

I used to spend hours wondering, why can't the world just be full of "thinkers?" Then we could all just get along. Is there anything really so wrong with "thinking?"

As you read this book, please be forewarned that if you succumb to the temptation to take even one little "think" along the way, it may forever alter your life.

If you're a non-thinker, you still have time. If you put this book down right now, you have a very good chance of continuing on in life in a relatively unruffled fashion. You don't have to endure the hardships that people with a "thinking" problem have to live with day in and day out.

But, then, maybe you're already a "thinker." If so, you're gonna eat this book up! Your brain, and heart are going to go on a virtual "thunkin" holiday. Let's dig in. Plop down somewhere comfortable and prepare to do some "serious thinking" together. In Isaiah 1:18 the Lord beckons us,

"Come now, let us reason (think) together......"

Thanks "Pat"

Introduction

Mankind has a pressing psychological need to explain the world;
It has no such need to see it explained correctly.

Patrick M. Morgan

This book contains brief answers to a collection of questions I have been asked over the years. They reflect a commonality of questions many people have had, and continue to have today. Hopefully you will find it to be a blessing. While traditionalists will concur with some of my answers, many of my views are non-traditional.

The answers I leave the reader with are synoptic and not exhaustive. In some cases, entire books could be, and have been, written to provide answers that I sum up in a few paragraphs. I apologize in advance to any critics who feel that I should have, or could have provided more substance or a better explanation to any particular question.

Paul said in Galatians 4:16 "Am I therefore become your enemy because I tell you the truth?"

Some of my answers may be upsetting. I have no *pressing psychological need* to upset people. I do however, have a need to get into the hands of honest seekers, viewpoints on scripture and Biblical issues that, in many cases up to this point, have been suppressed. I risk becoming an enemy to some, because I wish to be straight up about matters in the Bible that heretofore, have been in many cases, unintentionally or intentionally overlooked or covered-up. Who is responsible for the cover-up?

Mostly its well-meaning people that are merely denominationally dumbed down. They don't know, and they don't know that they don't know. In other cases, there are people that, in my opinion, are willing to go along, in order to get along, and in short, love the praise of men rather than the praise of God.

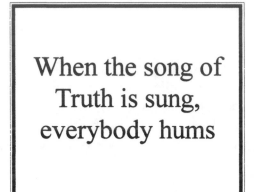

When the song of Truth is sung, everybody hums

I fear, that because some of my views are so non-conventional, some of my preacher friends may feel like I am picking on them. Believe me; at my age I am not interested in picking on anyone for any reason. I truly value all my ministerial friendships. I can honestly say I have benefited from every relationship I have ever had with each and every person spanning the entirety of my life.

If you like your thinking challenged, get <u>Without Controversy Volume II.</u> (Isn't that shameless) If you think I am way off base on some issue, call me. I'm always open to criticism or new insights. If God has given you a revelation from his Word, please, I beg of you, do not keep it to yourself.   If you are a preacher and have been thinking about something lately and fear that sharing your thought with a fellow minister will get you branded as a radical, liberal, or some other weird creature, please believe me, when I say, you can trust me. I've been there. I know what it's like to ponder a special question and have absolutely no one to confer with, for fear of the hot branding iron of social rejection being applied.

I preach things today I never taught, or in some cases even thought about, ten years ago. I have gone to my wonderful Church in Adrian and have had to confess that, on some points I previously taught as doctrine twenty years ago, I now, truly believe myself to have been in error. To my surprise, rather than their thinking me to be incompetent or reprobate, they have further embraced me as their spiritual leader. Their confidence has increased, because they feel that I can be trusted to tell them the truth. They also know, that if in the future I discover any additional error on some point of doctrine, that I will not hesitate to come forward as quickly as possible and correct the error.

The Church also seems to appreciate the fact, that if there is more than one view, or prevailing opinion of a particular doctrinal point, their pastor will try to present all sides of the issue in the interest of full disclosure. It's a kind of, "I report, you decide" relationship.

If you are a preacher, believe me when I say, people are not dumb, truth has a definite ring. Whether a bar-tender or a prostitute, a college professor, or shop foreman, when the song of Truth is sung, everybody hums. Jesus' sheep hear his voice, and another's they will not.

Remember, Patrick Morgan said, "Mankind does not have a pressing need to have the world explained correctly." But, we as ministers, have a duty to endeavor to present it correctly, even if it is not accepted. Jesus our great example knows how it is.

"Jesus came unto his own, and his own received him not....." John 1:11

There's only one Bible. Why are there so many denominations?

That's what I'd like to know. I don't see how an honest reading of the scriptures can come up any other view than that held by the Apostles and presented by the New Testament. When attempting to answer the question as to why so many denominations, it is important to consider the political situation of Christ's day.

The Roman Empire was the prevailing world government and it fully intended to maintain that position. The Jewish priests were uptight about the many people embracing Jesus and thus leaving the control of the Jewish religion. The newborn and rapidly expanding Church was radically gaining converts who confessed they had another king, one named Jesus.

"The rulers of the city were troubled when they heard theses things." (Acts 17:8)

These factors, combined to bring about prolonged periods of persecution. Some of these persecutions are recorded in the Bible, and more are found in historical writings like Foxes Book of Christian Martyrs.

The tension between Roman rulers, the Church and the Jewish priests who were religiously losing a grip on the people due to temple defections, grew and increased until the collapse of the Roman Empire. At that point a religious/political monstrosity driven by a company of former Jewish priests, who were followers of Christ but with a strong tendency to go back to the traditions of the Law, emerged from the chaos. In this time of political turmoil, an apostate political/religious entity seized the moment and declared itself to be the embodiment of Christ and wasted no time in solidifying its position in history as the single and official church.

Today, we know this revived Roman Empire as the Roman Catholic Church. For more than a thousand years, the Catholic Church, with its educated leadership, expanded and maintained control of the relatively uneducated masses of people. Historically speaking, it was the recognized Church, even though its ritual and teachings included things clearly not in the Bible. Such things as a three person divided godhead, Purgatory, the worship of Mary, prayers to the saints, sprinkling and infant baptism, and a ton of Old Testament style ritualistic practices like incense burning, confessing to a priest and more, were just a few of the matters that eventually led to a major split within the Catholic Church. The Leader of the split or reformation, as it came to be known, was a Catholic priest named Martin Luther.

Martin Luther, who referred to the Catholic Church as the synagogue of Satan, "protested" nearly a hundred of the practices of the Roman church. From his initial protest, the name Protestant was born. Luther was the first of the Protestants. He certainly wasn't the last. After Luther, with his mighty revelation that we are saved by grace and faith in Christ alone plus nothing else (like the sales of absolutions, a kind of free pass to sin) came others like Calvin, the Wesley Brothers, and many more.

Coincidental to this time the printing press was invented and the Bible was the first book printed in mass. Printing presses put the Bible in the hands of more and more common people further spreading the protestant reformation. Study of the newly printed Bibles brought to light even more revelations of truth heretofore hidden from the people. Baptism by immersion as opposed to sprinkling was one of the many revealed truths that soon became apparent. A new group of people who saw the truth of full immersion baptism and embraced it, came to be known as the Anna-Baptists (literally = re-baptizers)

With each new revelation of truth came a new wave of believers who often memorialized the name of their founding religious revolutionary, within the denominational name that continued after their demise. Luther birthed the Lutherans, Wesley the Wesleyans etc.

Although, there are literally hundreds of denominations today it is amazing how much of their doctrine is similar. For instance, the doctrine of the Trinity, formulated in the 4th century by the Church of Rome, which views God as a kind of divine committee is nearly universal amongst the denominational churches. Amazingly, the word trinity appears nowhere in scripture. While the word trinity, together with its definition of God being three persons, co- equal, co-eternal, and co-existent is not found in scripture; this fact is largely of no concern to many modern-day Christians.

Incidentally, while many political scientists fixate on the growth of the New World Order and one world government, the Church of Rome has never ceased in its diligence to bring as many denominational churches "back into the fold" by way of its ecumenical movement. The ecumenical movement is a mechanism to reconsolidate a single universal church. Catholicism has long taught that when Christ returns there will be only one Church, the Roman Catholic Church. A revived Roman world order of its own.

It is interesting to note that if you have been baptized in the titles Father, Son and Holy Ghost and thus embrace the mark of the trinity doctrine, you need not be re-baptized to become Catholic. However, if you have been baptized in the most excellent name above all names - Jesus Christ, the old Roman church will reject you and insist that you be re-baptized in the titles to become Catholic. I must tell you it gives me a great sense of satisfaction to know that Rome rejects me and my baptism, just as it did my savior Jesus Christ 2000 years ago.

If the Lord is a god of Love, then why does he allow so much evil? Couldn't he just do something about it?

Sure he could, but, that would require him to violate his own law and thus become unjust and unqualified to be our God. In addition to that, he would take away from us a wonderful thing. Freedom!

God made us in his image, a little lower than the angels. We are in effect, junior gods. We are not robots.

We are a reflection of his image. He has all power. We have limited powers. He has all knowledge. We have certain intellectual capacities. He sees all. We have eyes and have vision. He hears all. We have ears with which to hear. God decided to create a world and put us in it with creative and decision making abilities of our own and then turned us loose.

Unfortunately, Adam and Eve created and set in motion a domino effect of sin that continues unto this day. All this junk we have to put up with in this world was not God's idea. Adam and Eve, with their violation of divine order, set in motion the series of events which have culminated in the resulting world we find ourselves in today.

Every action evokes a re-action. Even the acts of the ancients in history, affect us today. We quite literally have to reap what they sowed.

"...by one man's disobedience (Adam's) many (all of us) were made sinners....." (Romans 5:19)

When I was a little kid I often got myself into trouble that my father would have to get me out of. In a similar way, Adam got us all into a jam that he could not get us out of. We, on earth, needed the grace and intervention of our Almighty Father. God has provided a way out of this mess for us, at the cross, through his salvation.

In the same way that prior decisions and acts got us to where we are at today, so, will it also require, conscience decisions and deliberate positive acts on our part to change our present course, that is, if we desire change.

Think of this life as a conveyor belt and you were just dropped on it. You find yourself on an already set stage with a host of situations you have no control over.

Look around you, everything is in motion, constantly changing. Bound by the law of time, there's no way to stop the conveyor.

But, know this, God did not predetermine the way the world should go. Mankind has literally been calling all the shots.

The Lord is a God of Love. He truly only wants what's best for you. That's why he came to earth two thousand years ago and did what he did at the cross. He willingly moved among us. God in the form of man, subjecting himself to the very world in which we live in order to make a way of escape for us.

Before you or I were even born, way back up the conveyor belt of time, God's loving remedy was already in place. God's plan of redemption was already in motion and was in the process of being promoted and publicized around the world. We call it preaching the good news of the gospel.

Jesus said, " You shall know the truth and the truth shall make you free." (John 8:32)

Just reading this book is getting truth and understanding into your mind. Your level of freedom is rising by the moment. Thoughts precede actions! I believe you're about to do something today that will affect you for a long time.

"As in Adam all die, so in Christ shall all be make alive." (I Corinthians 15:22)

God made you a "little creator" in his image. Now, go out and create a new future for yourself and those you love. You have the power to change your world. He made you in his image. Rejoice!

How do you know when you are born again?
What do I have to do ?

This is the very same question that was asked on the day of Pentecost, recorded in the Bible, in the Book of Acts 2:37, nearly 2000 years ago. People just like you, that wanted to be saved, asked "....what shall we do?"

The second chapter in Acts records the initial outpouring of Christ' Spirit into the lives of the first believers. A huge crowd had gathered together hearing the believers speaking in tongues, and wanted to know what was going on. Peter stood up and preached the true identity of the Lord Jesus Christ together with his death, burial and resurrection. As he preached, the full realization of who Jesus was formed in their minds, causing the people to ask, "Men and brethren, what shall we do?" (Acts 2:37)

In 2000 years, the question has not changed. Its been asked by millions of serious seekers, and you, just asked it again. If the question has never changed, doesn't it stand to reason the answer would never change either? Therefore, my answer to your question, is the same as the one Peter gave on that day. Peter said, "Repent and be baptized every one of you in the name of Jesus Christ for the remission of sin, and you shall receive the gift of the Holy Ghost. (Acts 2:38)

This is the fulfillment of Jesus' command to Nicodemus in John 3: 3-5 . "You must be born again of water and Spirit." Everywhere, throughout the Book of Acts, where people were born again, they were born of water and Spirit. Water baptism with Spirit baptism constituting being born again is found in Acts 2:1-39, Acts 8:12-16, Acts 10: 44-48, and Acts 19:1-6

Prayerfully consider the scriptures I have given you. Then, don't waste any time in getting baptized, and join with us in the great work of reaching the unsaved of this world.

Just who was Jesus Christ? Some people say he was God, but, how can that be?

Some people have a hard time with this one. We tend have a picture in our heads of God being a kind of Superman or Santa Claus figure, sitting on a throne up in heaven somewhere with a little boy (the son) and an elusive dove/spirit flying around. Together these three make up a "divine committee" that is called the godhead.

The problem is, this kind of imagery is found in mythology, not in the Bible.

The Bible declares that God is a spirit. (John 4:24) His spirit is invisible, fills all space, is all knowing, and has all power. The only way you can see the invisible God is to see the body that his spirit inhabits.

Jesus Christ was the "fullness of the Godhead Bodily." (Colossians 2:9) Jesus told Philip "When you have seen me, you have seen God." (John 14:8,9).

John 1:10 declares this about Jesus, "He was in the world and the world was made by him." Who made the world? "In the beginning God created the heavens and the earth" (Genesis 1:1)

Paul said, "And without controversy great is the mystery of godliness: God was manifest in the Flesh..." (I Timothy 3:16)

" For there are three that bear record in heaven, the Father, the Word, and the Holy Ghost; and these three are one." (I John 5:7)

Is it that important to believe that Jesus is God? Jesus said, "...For if you believe not that I am he, ye shall die in your sins." (John 8:24)

Why do some people make such a big deal about speaking in tongues, as if you've just got to do it?

I'm not sure what you mean by "making such a big deal" about speaking in tongues. It was commonplace in the book of Acts. Acts 2:4 says they were <u>all filled with the Holy Ghost</u> and began to speak in tongues.

It was universal in Acts. All of the initial converts spoke in tongues. In Acts 8:14-17 Peter made a special trip to visit the newly baptized believers at Samaria, specifically praying for them to receive the Holy Ghost and when they laid hands on them, they spoke in tongues. The Italians spoke in tongues in Acts 10:44-48 and the believers in Ephesus did in Acts 19: 1-6. Paul thanked God that he spoke in tongues, I Corinthians 14:18. And many more references to the phenomenon of speaking in tongues are made by Paul elsewhere.

I'm wondering if speaking in tongues is new to you. Perhaps you have never heard someone actually speak in tongues as the Spirit of God gives them the ability. Often times when something is new to us, we automatically tend to be wary or suspicious. If this is the kind of concern you have, I totally understand.

Frankly there are a lot of things in the Bible that don't make a lot of sense to common, ordinary, logical thinking people. A few examples include, Jesus spitting in dirt and putting it in a blind man's eyes to give him sight, Old Testament circumcision that brought sharp dissent, going to war with trumpets and candles causing walls to come crashing down. Washing the disciples feet, donkey's that talk with man's voice, painting your house with blood at the first Passover, and dipping oneself in the Jordan river to cure leprosy are all examples of events, together with results, that defy logic. How about Jesus' statement that unless you eat his flesh and drink his blood you have no life in you? The list could go on and on, with Biblical cites that leave the logically-minded reader with his head shaking.

" For as the heavens are higher than the earth, so are my ways higher than your ways, and my thoughts than your thoughts." (Isaiah 55:9)

> The handy thing about speaking in tongues is, I don't have to explain to people why I don't.

His ways are different than our ways. God doesn't consult with me or anyone else, that I know of, before he does something. The Lord is sovereign and can cause anyone to speak or not speak as he chooses.

"Tongues are for a sign" (I Corinthians 14:22.) In Acts 10:44 they knew they had the Holy Ghost "...for they heard them speak in tongues." It was the initial sign that Christ had filled them with his Spirit.

Isaiah 28:11,12 declares, " with stammering lips and another tongue will he speak to this people......yet they would not hear." Not understanding something that is new is one thing. But, Isaiah indicates that the problem with tongues was not that people would have questions, but rather, the people simply, "would not hear." In my experience with people who have an objection to speaking in tongues, the latter seems to be the prevailing attitude. I hope that is not the case with you.

I have a good friend who happens to be a Baptist preacher. One day we were talking about these Biblical questions as we stood at a table laden with some very elaborate tracts all written in an attempt to explain away the wonderful experience of the Holy Ghost with speaking in tongues. These tracts had interesting titles like, "Tongues Not For Us Today" "Tongues a Spirit of the Devil" and so on. As I looked at the tracts, the Lord gave me a very simple thought and so, without a moments hesitation, I shared it with my friend. I said, " You know Bill, there's one thing that's handy about speaking in tongues." Bill asked, "What's that?" I replied, " I don't have to explain to people why I don't."

Again, I really don't think we make a big deal about speaking in tongues. It just happens. Often times, when we baptize a new convert in Jesus Name, they come out of the water just like in the Bible - speaking in other tongues. I'm not an expert on how or why God does what he does. I just know it happens. And, If you get baptized in Jesus Name you'll probably come out of the water speaking in tongues too!

If Jesus said to baptize in the Name of the Father, Son and Holy Ghost, why did Peter command to be baptized in the Name of Jesus Christ? Isn't that a contradiction?

Peter knew that the NAME of the Father, Son and Holy Ghost was Jesus. His baptizing in the singular name of Jesus was a *fulfillment* of Christ's command to baptize in the name, not a *contradiction.*

Matthew 28:19 reads, "Go ye therefore and teach all nations baptizing them in the name of the Father, and of the Son, and of the Holy Ghost." Notice that the object of the sentence is the NAME. *Of the Father,* is a prepositional phrase which points back to and modifies, the name. The same is true of the phrase *of the Son.* It also is a prepositional phrase that modifies the NAME. Do you agree that the name of the Son is Jesus?

What if Matthew 28:19 only said, "baptizing them in the name of the Son?" Would it make sense to you that Peter in Acts 2:38 would command to be baptized in the name of Jesus Christ? Sure it would. In that case, the NAME of Jesus would be crystal clear. Just carry the logic through. Does the Father have a name? Jesus said, "I am come in my father's name" (John 5:43) and further, that the Comforter or the Holy Ghost would be sent "in my name." (John 14:26)

Paul said in I Corinthians 1:14-15 "I thank God that I baptized none of you, but Crispus and Gaius Lest any should say that I had baptized in mine own name." Here, it is abundantly clear that when baptisms took place, they involved the invoking of a proper name. They weren't baptized in the name of Paul. They were baptized in the Name of Jesus.

Philippians 2:9, makes the significance of the name so clear.

"Wherefore God also hath highly exalted him, and given him a name which is <u>above every name</u>." Any name, other than Jesus Christ, is an inferior name. Jesus is the name above every name. Have you been baptized in the Name of Jesus?

The book of Acts is consistent with every person being baptized in the name of Jesus. Nowhere in the Bible were the words Father, Son or Holy Ghost ever invoked. Nor were they intended to be. Father, Son and Holy Ghost are titles, not names. I am a father, a son, and a husband. Those are some of my titles, but not my name. I only have one name and so does the Savior. Acts 4:12 states clearly, "Neither is there salvation in any other, there is none other name under heaven, given among men whereby we must be saved. Jesus Christ is the saving name.

Some people have rather ignorantly said, "I'd rather follow the words of Jesus than Peter." To which I reply, I would too! But, do you realize, that in saying that, you are suggesting that there was some kind of miscommunication within the Kingdom of God with the Lord and his chosen disciples? If Peter was able to spend forty days with Christ after the resurrection, wherein Jesus spoke with his disciples the "things concerning the Kingdom of Heaven" (Acts 1:3) and not get it right on Pentecost, the birthday of the Church...... we are all in big trouble.

Jesus told Peter in Matthew 16:19 "....... whatsoever thou shalt *bind* in earth shall be *bound* in heaven." Peter's sermon on the day of Pentecost recorded in Acts 2 concluded with an offer of a contract to the people to have their sins set aside (remitted) and be in covenant with God. Peter was the initial agent, if you will, who carried the good news to the people that a legally *binding* covenant was now open and offered freely to "those who gladly received his word." (Acts 2:41)

Three thousand souls entered the contract that day. And millions more have followed. Acts 2:38 was valid and binding on that day and is still open for your acceptance today.

Lastly, consider Acts 19, where Paul found certain disciples who had <u>already been baptized</u>, but, were willingly re-baptized on the spot. In the first baptism, they were baptized unto John's baptism, but Acts 19:4 says, "when they heard this," they were re-baptized in the name of the Lord Jesus. In both cases they had been immersed in water. Nothing changed in the mode of baptism. The only thing that was different, was what was pronounced over the convert being immersed. The Name of Jesus Christ made the difference.

"One Lord, one faith, <u>one baptism</u>." (Eph 4:5)

I indicated earlier, that Jesus came in his father's name. Some will point out that the Old Testament name of God is YHWH which has an approximate pronunciation of Yahweh. The Lord has included his name in a variety of Old Testament names like Jeremi-yah, Obedi-yah, Hezeki-yah and so, it is fitting that the Son's name, reflects the Father's. Our Savior's Hebrew name is Yahshua which literally means "Yah" has become "Shuah" (our salvation.) "The word was made flesh and dwelt among us." (John 1:14)

Some further argue, that if the Savior's Hebrew name is Yahshua, then, why not use it, instead of the greek/latin transliteration of Jesus? Good question.

I know a pastor in Texas, who, after pastoring a large Pentecostal church for many years, and having always baptized, and preached in Jesus name, felt led that it would be more Biblical to use the Hebrew names when ministering and to include the name of Yahshua when baptizing..

He started using the name of Yashua in place of Jesus, largely when teaching, preaching and praying. This was done for a period of about six months and during that time something very strange happened. His once, Spirit-charged church, lost its vibrancy and he, lost his anointing to preach the way he was accustomed to.

I suppose, if you are not familiar with truly Spirit-filled, Holy Ghost anointed worship, what I am trying to relate to you may be hard to grasp. Pastor Foster said, that in just six months time, he and his Church, completely lost their anointing. It was hard to understand, when after all, they were striving so hard to honor God's true revealed and Biblically verifiable name. Why had the once vibrant and spiritually charged and passionate Church body gone virtually dead?

In the light of historical Biblical research, linguistics, and every sense of logic, the name of Jesus was never used by Peter, Paul or any of the first century Christians, and yet, in some otherwise unexplainable way, God chooses to honor the name of The Lord Jesus Christ, above every name.

Pastor Ron Poch said, "What other name does the devil hate? What other name do the traditional enemies of Christ blaspheme? It's not Yahshua. Extremist Jews who deny Christ, spit on the name of Jesus, not Yashua.

Pastor Foster said, "After six month, I determined to go back to using Jesus name, and the anointing of God's presence returned." I can't explain it, he said, "But I can tell you its true." There's just something about the Name of Jesus that makes all the difference.

I agree. For Hundreds of years, healings and innumerable deliverances have come through the name of Jesus, and millions have found remission of sins, through baptism in his name.

For more, refer to Acts 8:14-16, Acts 10:44-48, and Acts 19: 1-6

My pastor told me you don't have to do anything like get baptized to be saved. The thief on the cross never got baptized and he went to heaven with Jesus by just believing. What do you say to that?

The "thief on the cross" plays a prominent role of religious drama, within the minds of many who inhabit churchianity today. Your pastor's rationale that you refer to, is a testimony to the power of repetitive religious propaganda and the willingness of gullible people to follow non-biblical teachings.

Jesus said, "today you will be with me in paradise." It is assumed that this is somewhere in the world beyond, but the word paradise literally means a "park, or orchard." It in no way is translated heaven.

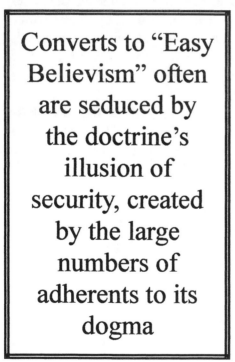

Converts to "Easy Believism" often are seduced by the doctrine's illusion of security, created by the large numbers of adherents to its dogma

When you read the specific dialog there is nothing in it that acknowledges forgiveness, remission of sin, or everlasting life. Wherever the paradise that Jesus was referring to was, is where he went, but there is no mention of his going to heaven. So, if your pastor told you the thief went to heaven, he is misstating what the scripture says. The thief went to Paradise.

This is one of the favorite scriptures of the "easy believers." "Easy Believers," are nice people who have participated in a plan of salvation that is not found in the Bible. Converts to this popular delusion, often are seduced by the doctrine's illusion of security, created by the large numbers of adherents to its dogma. If millions of people accept it, believe it and preachers preach it, how can "Easy Believism" be wrong? It's one of those strength in numbers games. (Remember, the world used to be flat....)

"Easy Believism" takes a number of scriptures out of context, reshuffles them and deals them out in such as way that faith in Christ and salvation is obtained by simply accepting what Christ did and believing. A purely mental exercise only, plus nothing. Plus nothing, means no baptism is required. Just believe.

Now, for the sake of argument, let's assume that the thief made his confession, and as a K-mart styled "blue light special," just before Christ died, the Lord extended a bonus of grace to one lone, down and out, 'bout to die sinner. Bingo, this is your lucky day Jack. Today, you go home with me to heaven.

That's a beautiful story. For the thief's sake, I hope that's exactly what happened. But whatever happened, it was a selective act of grace extended by the Savior, and has no relevance or bearing on anyone else but the thief. There are three main reasons why.

His salvation, if you will, was obtained prior to the establishment of the Church. Of course, the thief didn't need to be baptized. No one had been baptized for the remission of sins, yet. There was no gospel for anyone to respond to, yet. There was nothing for anyone to believe, yet. There was no "new" covenant, yet.

It was not until approximately seven weeks later on the day of Pentecost, when the Church was born, that the door to New Testament salvation was opened. Peter was the man with the keys. (Matt. 16:19) He opened the door in Acts 2:38. It was over seven weeks after the thief died on the cross and went to Paradise, wherever that is; that the Gospel of the Lord Jesus

Christ was authorized to be preached and the very first recipients of salvation entered into the body of Christ. Peter referred to that day as the "beginning" (Acts 11:15)

The beginning was <u>not at the cross</u>. The beginning was <u>not with the thief's confession of faith</u>. The beginning of New Testament salvation was with the first baptized converts (Acts 2:38-41.)

Even the "Easy Believer" favorite of Romans 10:9 doesn't fit with the thief.

"If thou shalt confess with thy mouth the Lord Jesus, **and shalt believe in thine heart that God hath raised him from the dead, thou shalt be saved.**" (Romans 10:9) The poor thief on the cross couldn't have known that Christ was going to be raised from the dead, much less believe it in his heart.

Furthermore, to try to justify simple lip confessions such as accepting the Lord as your personal savior and bypass baptism, and the receiving of Christ's' Spirit, is to make void the scripture that "God is no respecter of persons." (Acts 10:34) If what your preacher told you is true, then Ephesians 4:5 " there is one Lord, one faith, one baptism" is evidently false.

According to what your preacher says, there evidently is more than one Lord, more than one faith, and no baptism is necessary at all.

If all that was necessary to receive everlasting life and forgiveness of sin was a simple lip confession, like the thief, then the 3000 on the day of Pentecost and the others at Samaria, and Cornelius' house, and the Ephesians, did it all wrong. What they obeyed and participated in by repenting and being baptized in water and Spirit, was (according to your pastor) unnecessary. Jesus' command to go and baptize, was just a bunch of meaningless words. Also Mark 16:16 "He that believeth <u>and is baptized shall be saved</u>..."

is without meaning.

According to your pastor, much of the Bible is fraudulent and does not mean what it says. For instance, when Israel was delivered out of Egypt at Passover, they didn't need to sacrifice a lamb, apply the blood to the door post or do any of the other matters recorded for us in the book of Exodus. All they needed to do was believe. Your pastor's understanding of what happened with the thief on the cross seems to have given him an insight into salvation that makes the Bible unnecessary.

What makes more sense to you? God's repetitive, demonstrated example of thousands of sincere people (just like you) being baptized and filled with the Holy Ghost, recorded for your reading, in the Bible; or, a fanciful, "Easy Belief" exercise, that no one in the Book of Acts Church participated in.

The choice is yours. Jesus said, "You shall know the truth and the truth shall make you free."

This is an eternally serious matter. Why don't you pray right now and ask the Lord to show you the truth. I feel confident, that if you are sincere, he will give you a sure answer.

[**Special note**: "Easy Believing" has a "truth inoculating" effect. It injects a "skin-deep," minimum dosage of Jesus and thus "protects" the recipient from further infections of truth. Some adherents to "Easy Believe" are seemingly incapable of further spiritual enrichment because of this effect. When approached with the revelation of Acts 2:38 and Baptism in Jesus Name, the inoculation typically kicks in, with a knee jerk response of, "I don't need anything more, I'm already saved."

While I rejoice anytime someone's eyes are opened up to Christ, I am at the same time grieved and frustrated, if, their initial experience has the effect of stunting their possibility of further growth. Are you susceptible or immune to more truth?]

What does the Bible mean in Revelation 19:9 when it refers to the Marriage Supper of the Lamb?

The Bible is a love story.   Complete with courtship, marriage, infidelity, separation, divorce, and the possibility of remarriage.

The groom is the Lord. The bride is a nation called Israel.

In the beginning of the story, the Lord God had close communion with Adam and Eve in a beautiful place called the Garden of Eden.   Tragically, that special relationship was disrupted by the sin of disobedience. The rest of the Bible, from Genesis in the Old Testament, all the way through Revelation, the last book of the New Testament, is an unfolding of the romantic relationship that God had with his special creation.

The lineage between Adam and a man named Abraham was a very important one.   Through Abraham, God promised to create a special nation that would make his name great and be a blessing to the whole world.

In time, Abraham had a son named Isaac. Isaac had a son named Jacob.   Jacob's name was changed to Israel.   Jacob/Israel had twelve sons who became the heads of the twelve tribes of Israel.

Israel has had a very colorful and exciting history. Some of it was very dramatic and full of supernatural influences from God. The deliverance from Egypt, and occupation of the promised land are but a couple of the great happenings that Israel experienced when this nation had the favor of its God.

God declared that the relationship between himself and Israel was one of <u>husband and wife</u>. (Isaiah 54:5) God repeatedly warned Israel to be faithful and not to flirt with, or commit whoredom with, any other gods. But, as good as God was to his wife, and no matter how God tried to keep Israel faithful, the marriage was doomed to complete failure. Not on God's part of course. Israel just couldn't resist the urge to be unfaithful.

The marital relationship seriously floundered after Israel chose to be ruled by earthly Kings, rather than by God himself. The Kings were a predictable problem and in time, led to God's nation dividing into two nations. The larger nation consisted of ten tribes and was called Israel, the remaining, smaller fragment was called Judah.

In time, God would have no choice but to divorce Israel. God however, chose not to divorce Judah. This decision to keep the marital door open to Judah, was for a specific legal reason, as shall be seen at a little town called Bethlehem.

All through this tumultuous relationship, God never stopped loving Israel. He wrote love letters and had them delivered by way of prophets. He begged Israel to please come home. But, Israel could not be persuaded. Finally, when God divorced Israel, things went very badly for this lost and soon to be scattered nation.

Her enemies were able to enslave her. She lost her finest cities, and in time she even lost her name Israel and the identity of who she was. History lost track of Israel during her wanderings as well. The lost, cast-off, and scattered nation of Israelites appear variously in history under the assumed names of Celts, Normans, Basque, Lombards, Scythians, Angles, Saxons, Vikings, Franks, among others. At the time of Christ, they were largely known as Gentiles. Jesus called them his "lost or scattered sheep."

Many times, God would have loved to have taken Israel back as his bride, but God was legally forbidden to do so, because of a very specific clause in his marriage covenant.

The Law stipulated that once a divorce was final, the divorced mate who was sent out to marry another, could not later, after a change of heart, return and remarry the first party. (Deut. 24:1-4) With this stipulation, how could God ever have Israel back as a wife? Israel was divorced, and adulterous. God himself was now a party to a divorce. Could there possibly be a solution to this dilemma?

God was lonely and there was no way the love of his life could come back to him, even if she wanted to. Israel, like any other wife, was bound to the law of marriage until the death of her husband. God could never die, could he? If there was to be any hope for a future relationship with his lost love again, God would have to perform a very special work.

At the appropriate time, God came to Judah, whom he had not divorced and thus had a lawful marital right to approach. His Spirit came unto a virgin named Mary, who conceived a child, literally, an offspring of God called, the Son of God. The invisible creator put on a robe of visible flesh and went town to town, village to village, in order to seek and save that lost nation. That was God's only mission. The scripture says, Jesus was "not sent, but to the lost sheep of the house of Israel." The journey was depressing in so many ways. "God was in the world, the world was made by him and the world knew him not. He came to his own and his own received him not." (John 1: 10-11) One time he even wept and cried out loud,

"Oh Jerusalem, Jerusalem, which killest the prophets, and stonest them that are sent unto thee; how often would I have gathered thy children together, as a hen doth gather her brood under her wings, and you would not." (Luke 13:34)

In fact his ex-wife, Israel, rejected him so vigorously, they hanged him on a tree until he was dead. Israel was so depraved spiritually, she was unable to perceive who Jesus was. Indeed,

".... for had they known who he was, they would not have crucified the Lord of Glory." (I Corinthians 2:8) But, with Christ' death, something very interesting happened.

After dying, being buried and then rising from the dead, this God/Savior, named The Lord Jesus Christ, was literally born a new creation. God made a grand-opening on an entirely pristine new stage. His death, burial and resurrection had a profound and wonderful affect on his legal status. It had freed him from the remarriage prohibition clause contained in the law of divorce. Legally, his status was now equivalent to that of a man that had never been married.

What wonderful news! God is eligible to be married and he is actively seeking his bride.

But poor Israel, who had thrown her life quite literally away and became lost and scattered like sheep, was not qualified, because of her divorced status, to be married to God again unless she too, were able to die and be reborn or "born again." Well, that's exactly what she has been able to do since the day of Pentecost. (Acts 2)

Two thousand years ago messengers like the Apostle Peter and others, began to proclaim a special marriage invitation from the groom.

"Israel, your husband tasted death and has come back to life, thus making it possible for him to marry you." In your present state, you are unable to accept the marriage proposal, but......

You, too, can submit yourself to the same rebirthing process. You can die by repenting of your sin, you can then be buried by baptism, in a watery grave in the holy name of your every loving, always faithful, never wavering, constantly seeking, love-letter writing, blood washing, God and Savior. When you come out of

31

that symbolic grave, you will be given new life through the Spirit of your God and a part in the upcoming marriage. You too, can die, be buried, and rise to walk into the newness of life.

It is important for us to be patient. It may take some time until all who are bidden to the marriage, have an opportunity to receive their invitation. Messengers are tirelessly busy, seeking all over the world for Adam's scattered seed.. Someday, in the future though, it will be time for the marriage and its celebration to take place.

".... For the marriage of the Lamb is come, and his *wife* hath made herself ready..... Blessed are they which are called unto the *marriage supper of the Lamb*....." (Revelation 19:7)

"... I, John saw the holy city, new Jerusalem, coming down from God out of heaven prepared as a *bride* adorned for her *husband*..... ..there came unto me one of the seven angels ...saying, come hither I will show you the *bride, the Lambs wife*. ... and the angel showed me that great city, the holy Jerusalem descending out of heaven from God.....and on the walls ...names written which are the name's of the twelve tribes of the *children of Israel*.....and there shall in no wise enter into (the city) any thing... but they, which are written in the Lamb's book of life...." (Revelation 21::2,9,10,12,27.)

Is your name written in the Lambs Book of Life?

I've heard people say they talk with God. Are they just saying that, or is it possible?

Prayer is simply talking *to* God.

Talking *with* God implies that a *conversation* is taking place. Did anyone in the bible have two way conversations with God?

Adam and Eve clearly did. Noah did. Abraham did. Jacob wrestled and argued with the angel of the Lord saying "I have seen God face to face..." The prophets spoke for God.

In the New Testament Peter prayed and fell into a trance and in that state had a conversation with the Almighty. (Acts 10:10-17)

Paul was struck down by a powerful light and engaged a conversation with the Lord on the road to Damascus. (Acts 9:1-6) He even asked the specific identification of the heavenly speaker and was told, "I am Jesus, who you persecute..." Paul then asked, "What would you have me to do?" The Lord then told him what to do. That's a definite conversation with God.

John on the Isle of Patmos, wrote his one-way conversation down and we can read it in the Book of Revelation.

There are other instances we could cite. You may already be aware of these examples in the Bible. You want to know, do people today have such communion with the Lord?

The Apostles in Acts 15:28 are recorded as saying "...it seemed good to the Holy Ghost and to us,....." implying that in their prayer and deliberations they were in communication with God, but not necessarily in the same way in which you might be, if you used a telephone. Their contact with the other world was more of an impression. "It <u>seemed</u> good to the Holy Ghost."

33

I have certainly prayed and asked God's counsel and felt an impression one way or the other and I am satisfied that God and I were in communication. What actually takes place? Sometimes it almost seems like I am talking with myself and I realize I am engaging another voice somehow. Let me give you an example.

I was driving on an interstate highway one time when, as I passed a car, a little voice in my head said, "she (the driver) is not aware you are passing her." I watched carefully as she began to move into my lane. I beeped my horn and she quickly moved back. If I had not heard the voice, we quite probably could have at least had a bump in, if not a more serious accident. Is that God speaking to me?

Many times when I am in a quandary about what to do about a church matter, I simply ask the Lord in prayer and invariably it seems that an appropriate answer comes to me. Not necessarily a spoken, "burning bush" type of message, but still a definite impression as to what is the best way to go.

I distinctly remember the day that the U.S. Marshal came to the Church to serve me with an order to "show cause" in Federal Court, regarding our radio station. God didn't particularly give me any forewarning, but Martha, a fellow Christian, who was at the Church that day, came in the door and whisked past me on the way to the prayer room telling me that she felt an extremely heavy burden. She was visibly shaken and over-whelmed with a definite and somber demeanor. Not more than ten minutes later the Federal U.S. Marshals were at the door. Was God communicating a "code red" alert, an evil event is imminent, to this sister in the Lord? I definitely think so.

Where in the Bible does it say we have to "go to church?" I have communion with Christ in my home I don't need other people.

Hebrews 10:25 says, " Not forsaking the assembling of ourselves together as the manner of some is, ... And so much the more as you see the day approaching." It is apparent from the Bible and secular history, that the early Church "met together" at specific places and at predetermined times. They believed that the return of the Lord was near, even in their day. "The day approaching," could of course, include your personal day of departure as well as Christ' actual physical return.

Do you see the day of the Lord's return getting closer? Doesn't it seem Biblical to you that you should intensify your fellowship with believers and not forsake it, or neglect it?

It is not good for man to be alone.

Genesis 2:18

The Lord established his Church to be a "body." A living organism.
Complete with eyes, ears, hands and feet. The Church is literally Christ in the earth.

He gave up his personal, single, physical body, in order to pour himself into a limitless and ever growing global body.

Paul addressed some of where you seem to be coming from in I Corinthians 12: 12-31 where he describes the body as being made up of different parts with differing significance. Paul writes, the eye cannot say to the hand "I have no need of thee." Because the hand needs the eye, and the head need the feet and so on. So when you say you don't need the Church, it's apparent to me that you have a lack of understanding of what the divine purpose of

35

the Church is.

At the same time, I can fully appreciate the fact that you may be one of those people who has had a bad experience with a particular brand of churchianity, that left a bad or bitter taste in your mouth and what you are really saying is, you don't need "that" church. I understand. But don't let that "one bad experience" keep you from pursuing the true will of God for your life. Believe me, "it is not good for man to be alone..." Family, community, nationhood, the Church, - it is all meant by God to be interconnected and interdependent in a Biblical way.

You need the interconnectedness, spiritually and emotionally, that can only be found within a good Spirit-filled and Word-directed Church. I pray the Lord shows you one today.

When do you think the Rapture will occur?

What Rapture? I have never found the word Rapture in the Bible.

I am not sure how to answer your question. You might simply be referring to the promised return of Jesus. Or, you might be referring to the "Hal Lindsey" modernist idea of people disappearing in a flash of time and shooting up through holes in the sky, to later return in a secondary second coming of Christ. Which event are you talking about?

If your question is simply about Christ's return to the planet to establish his reign on earth, nobody knows the time. The time for all those matters is clearly within the Father's prerogative. However, the Father definitely has set a time for all things. Notice the wording of Acts 2. "Now when the day of Pentecost was *fully come......*" The Holy Spirit arrived right on time. The day was "fully come." So will Christ's return be right on time, in the fullness of time.

Consider the heavens, the precise and predictable movements of the earth around the sun and the phases of the moon. God is all about time. The Lord set a big celestial clock in motion when he did the creation and he keeps perfect time. The return of the Lord will be right at the specific, predetermined moment, not a second sooner or later.

However, there is a significant difference in the promise of Christ's return, and a concept that is popularly referred to as the Rapture. They are two mutually exclusive things altogether.

It's interesting to note that the teaching of the Rapture doctrine is not a very old one. It first surfaced in 1830. None of the reformist writers like Wyclif, Huss, Calvin Knox, Zwingli, Tyndale, Foxe, Newton, Calvin, Luther, or the Wesley brothers speak of it. Don't be confused. <u>They spoke of the return of Christ</u>, but they never spoke of a mystical disappearance through holes in the sky event, like the "Rapture fever crowd" does today.

While European Christians are less caught up in this doctrine, the allure of the rapture has a definite appeal to people in America. Americans hate pain, inconvenience and misery. Accordingly, the "escape and by-pass misery" feature of the Rapture has a natural appeal.

II Timothy 4:3 "For the time will come when men will not put up with sound doctrine. Instead, to suite their own desires, they will gather around them a great number of teachers to say what their itching ears want to hear. They will turn their ears away from the truth and *turn aside to myths*" NIV. Myths like the rapture???

Corrie ten Boom said, "The Rapture doctrine is a false teaching that Jesus warned us to expect in the latter days," (Logos Journal, November,- December 1974 P. 20)

The Rapture doctrine lines up selected scriptures and adds a special twist. As a package, it is designed to convince you that at a specific time, before things get too bad here on earth, Jesus will appear in the clouds and whisk all the believers away instantaneously, in a flash of time. No one knows when the Rapture is to occur, and thus you must always be ready for it. The occurrence of the Rapture constitutes the Lord's initial second coming.

After hell on earth (the tribulation) is over, Christ returns a second time, (really a second second coming) with his Raptured ones, he then, sets foot on the mount of Olives and stays on earth to set up his kingdom.

Biblically, it is undeniable that Christ has promised to return to earth, that the dead in Christ will be resurrected, the saved living will be glorified together with them, and that his people will rule and reign with him. The wicked will be judged, and everyone found written in the Lambs Book of Life shall forever be with the Lord. You can count on all of this.

But, the Rapture really puts a whole different spin on future events. In my opinion, the Rapture teaching is not only error, but it is also counter-productive.

Here's how. The Rapture proponents are big on hyping the sneak attack feature of its occurrence. You never know when it will happen, so you better act fast! While I agree that there is no time like the present to prepare to meet the Lord, scaring adults and little children into the kingdom is not consistent with the mode of either Christ, or the Apostles. Shameless preaching that puts mental images in the minds of little children of mommy and daddy vanishing and leaving them behind with the devil, has, in the past, scurried plenty of anguishing and horrified kids to the altar, that's for sure. But, is that the kind of method Jesus used when he said, "suffer the little children to come unto me?"

Whatever happened to "charity never fails?" Does the Rapture teaching win people over to Christ' love or just put a fear and panic in their hearts that they better get it while its hot or else? I know from personal experience how damaging fear tactics can be. My own children were damaged by it, and it has taken years to repair the damage, and help them reestablish a loving and worshipful relationship with the one who hung between two thieves.

Secondly, the Rapture appeals to escapists. Rapture fever proponents insist the Lord has not appointed us to wrath. Before the Anti-Christ can get us, the rapture will save the day. Or, so they claim.

Alright, what makes you and I think we are so special to the

Lord? Have you ever read Foxes Book of Martyrs? What do you say to all the hundreds of thousands of Christian believers who have already experienced death, dismemberment, tortures and other persecutions simply because they embraced the name of Jesus? What would you say to them? You wouldn't need to say anything. They had never heard of the so-called Rapture. They were simply so committed to the Savior, that they preferred death at the hands of their wicked persecutors, rather than to escape torture and live life as a Christ denier. Jesus said, "Be thou faithful unto death, and I will give you a crown of life." (Revelation 2:10) Which brings me to my next point.

If your faith in Christ is based on the promise of an escape before things get too bad, then what will happen to your faith, somewhere along the line, if things get worse and worse and no Rapture takes place?   My guess, is that when hell on earth intensifies, people who are heavily invested in the Rapture may start questioning everything else they have been told by the preacher or their church. The Rapture, if it does not occur, may rapidly destroy faith.

Additionally, the Rapture teaching is a doctrine that encourages irresponsibility. Christians by the millions in America, refuse to get involved in the political process by not voting or otherwise working to improve and protect the wonderful country we live in, because after all, what's the use? The Rapture will be taking place soon and we'll all be gone. Why work to improve something that the Lord has already declared shall "wax worse and worse..."

Some scholars maintain, that China fell to the Communists, due, in large part, to Chinese Christian ministers telling the people not to resist the Communists, because the Rapture would take place soon and they would all be delivered. Thus, the people who should have been best suited to resist the Satanic and murderous Communists, did nothing, and China fell into demonic slavery.

Don't get me wrong! I am a strong proponent of the return of our Savior. I hope to see it in my lifetime. But the twisting of scripture to make a Rapture scenario work out, while at the same time instilling a lazy and irresponsible mode of thinking into the believer, is doctrinally dishonest and inconsistent with Christ's commission.

Jesus prayed, "Father, <u>do not take them out of the world</u> but keep them from evil" (John 17:15)

The Psalmist seems to describe something like a rapture, but it is clearly for the *wicked,* not the righteous. "Let the sinners be consumed out of the earth, and let the wicked be no more." (Psalm 104:35) "God shall likewise destroy thee (the wicked) forever; He shall *take thee away* and *pluck thee out (rapture?)* of thy dwelling place." (Psalm 52:5)

Proverbs 10:30 is in direct contrast to Rapture teaching. "The righteous *shall never be removed,* and the wicked shall not inhabit the earth."

Revelation 9:3 "..... and unto them (locusts) was given power, as the scorpions of the earth have power. And it was commanded them, that they should not hurt the grass of the earth, neither any green thing, neither any tree; but only those who *do not have the (mark) seal of God on their foreheads.*" Those without the mark of God co-exist with the righteous who do have the mark of God.

God's people go nowhere during the last days of time. We are "...hid with God in Christ." (Colossians 3:3) But we are not going anywhere.

I Thessalonians 4:17 speaks of the return of Christ with the dead in Christ being resurrected and all believers being joined with the "Clouds" of witnesses, (Hebrews 12:1) in the "Air," meaning the atmosphere above ground, not in the grave or under the earth. Furthermore, we are told "so we shall ever be with the Lord." We will be with him, on earth, consistent with the scriptures - not transformed into sky rockets through the clouds.

In closing, I would like to encourage you to do something, if you wouldn't think me too presumptuous. Please stop using non-Biblical terms like the Rapture, or the Trinity. The critics of Christian faith just love it when they can make us look stupid or incompetent by calling our hands when our resource of words or teachings are clearly not Biblical. Start right now and determine to discipline yourself to strive to be as Biblical as possible in all things.

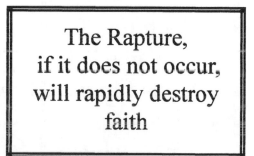

The Rapture, if it does not occur, will rapidly destroy faith

At this time, there is a very popular book and movie series out called, "I Don't Want To Be Left Behind." It is a fictional work that depicts how horrible it will be on earth after the Rapture. Millions of otherwise sensible Christians are just nuts about it.

A friend of mine, Pastor Ron Poch, has recently authored a book which was written to respond to the current hysteria caused by the Left Behind fever. Ron's excellent book is called "I Want To Be Left Behind." You will be fascinated by his excellent research. Reading Ron Poch's book makes it clear that the Rapture teaching is a pure, non-Biblical, money-making, fantasy.

What do you think of women preaching, and what does the Bible say about it?

This could be a touchy subject for me because my wife preaches and is very active in our local body. Just kidding. I think your question is a good one. But I'm not sure if you are asking about women serving as pastors, or just women preaching or speaking in the congregation. In my mind there's a big difference.

The primary Biblical standard for all leadership in this world is, a man, who is scripturally submitted to God's order. "The head of the woman is the man, the head of the man is Christ, the head of Christ is God." I Corinthians 11:3. That's the order God set up. Therefore, women in the status of judges, bosses, foreman etc. over the man is scripturally out of order, accordingly, the office of pastor should be held by a male of God's choosing.

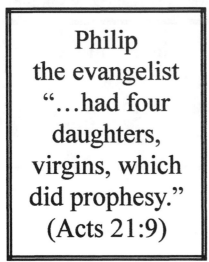

Philip the evangelist "...had four daughters, virgins, which did prophesy." (Acts 21:9)

However, there are, in my view, a few temporary exceptions to the general rule (as there usually is) that I believe God accepts. One exception could be, if a church's pastor were to die and his wife temporarily stepped in to preside over the business of the church until an appropriate replacement for the pastor could be arranged. Another might be if there simply was no man qualified to pastor, a woman could substitute temporarily until God provided a man pastor. While we are considering exceptions to the rule, this is probably why Deborah is noted as a judge in Israel for a period of time. She is the only woman identified as a judge. She was definitely an exception to the rule. How she came to be a judge is not revealed in the text.

In the New Testament we find some insights into the question of the woman's role. From I Timothy 3:2 The qualifications for a bishop include that he be "the *husband* of one wife." How could a woman be the husband of one wife? Verse 4 "... one that ruleth *his* house well." These scriptures are obviously referring to men.

All the Apostles, chosen by Christ, were men. Christ chose no women for *leadership* roles. All this substantiates what most people know by nature to be true. However, women certainly have Biblical roles that are vocal, instructive, and side by side with men. Such was the case with Philip the evangelist who "...had four daughters, virgins, which did prophesy." (Acts 21:9) .

Acts 16:1 "Phebe our sister which is a servant of the Church which is at Cenchrea." Phebe was a notable person in the Church according to Paul. One could assume she also spoke. The same would be true of the role played by Aquilla with Pricilla. Let's not forget what was prophesied by Joel and repeated by Peter in his message preached on the day of Pentecost Acts 2:17 " ...and your sons and *daughters* shall prophesy..." Luke 2:36 mentions a godly woman, "Anna a prophetess...... and (she) *spoke* of him to all them that looked for redemption in Jerusalem." Anna was a speaker.

I conclude, woman certainly have been teachers and speakers in a variety of capacities in the Church. They are not to usurp authority over the man. (I Timothy 2:12) But, within the Biblical parameters I mention above, women obviously have a definite and necessary role to play.

What does the Bible say about divorce and re-marriage?

The Bible is pretty clear on the grounds for divorce. Adultery gives an out to the unoffending party to be free of the marriage. Marriage is a covenant or contract between a man, a woman, and God. When one party is in material breach, the other innocent party is not obligated to further perform, and may option to dissolve the agreement. Where the big zone of mystery lies, is on the question of the re-marriage of either or both of the original parties to a marriage that dissolved into divorce.

I want to start by saying that although some preachers feel like they have it all figured out on this matter of divorce and re-marriage - they don't. The scriptures are just not clear and definitive enough on this subject. I have listed the bulk of the scriptures which relate to this question. After perusing them, you will have a better understanding of why there is so much controversy and imprecision within this subject.

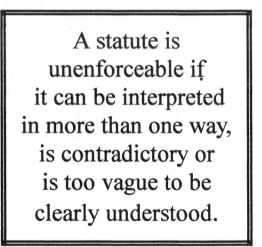

A statute is unenforceable if it can be interpreted in more than one way, is contradictory or is too vague to be clearly understood.

Putting away a wife without adultery - causes her to commit adultery. Whoever marries a divorced woman commits adultery. (Matt 5:32)

Divorce without just cause and marrying another causes the other to commit adultery. (Matt 19:9)

Whoever divorces his wife and marries another commits adultery. (Mark 10:11)

If a woman divorces her husband and marries another she commits adultery. (Mark 10:12)

The man and the woman he committed adultery with shall be executed. (Lev. 20:10)

Committing adultery destroys your soul. (Proverbs 6:32)

Looking on a woman to lust after her, is the same as adultery in your heart. (Matthew 5:28)

If a man marries a woman and discovers some "uncleanness" (uncleanness, as used here, has no precise meaning. Some speculate it means anything from a deformity to a lack of virginity) he can give her a bill of divorcement and send her out of his house. Afterward he and she are both able to marry. (Deut. 24:2)

If a man divorces his wife and she marries another, who either divorces her or he dies thus leaving her single again, her original husband may not take her for his wife again. (Duet. 24:2-4) (See also Marriage Supper of the Lamb.)

Do you begin to see why there is no clear and concise answer to the question of divorce and remarriage?

The way Jesus explains the entire divorce subject, it is clear, that from the beginning, God meant every marriage to be a merging of two flesh into one and never any splitting up of the union. Moses evidently stepped out on his own in providing for legal divorce. (Refer to Mark 10:2-8)

This whole matter was obviously a controversy in Christ' day or it wouldn't have come up as often as it did, and from so many different people.

I wish to draw your attention to something that any of your lawyer friends will confirm. In our modern practice of law, a legal statute is unenforceable, if it can be interpreted in more than one way, is contradictory, or is too vague to be clearly understood. Truly, I have to believe this is one of those situations. In the great judgment hall in Heaven, if, before the Great Judge of eternity, I have to give any answers on behalf of anyone I know relative to the marriage, divorce and remarriage question, I will definitely make the "void for vagueness" argument, and hope the all-wise and just King is understanding. The defense I would make would be something like this.

"Your Majesty, O' King of Kings and Lord of Lords, we beg your indulgence and compassionate consideration upon this matter that has wreaked so much confusion within the minds of we mere mortals. As you are already aware, marriage, divorce, and re-marriage has been going on for thousands of years involving untold millions of people. By the time I got on the scene things were so messed up, I just tried to help people get their broken and mixed up lives reasonably back on course and then urge them to do the best they could.. You yourself, once made a most heart-moving exception to the letter of the Law with the pronouncement, to the woman taken in the very act of adultery, 'go and sin no more...' In a similar way, we ask your mercy.

Not everyone agrees with me. A number of conservative Christians take a very narrow, no re-marriage view. A few extremists might even tell you something like this.

"If you are divorced, that's it! You had your chance. You made a bad choice. We told you not to marry him, but no, you wouldn't listen...... Now your only hope is to remain single and hope that if you suffer loneliness with enough humility, maybe, just maybe, on the day your sorry soul dies, the Lord may allow you in the Pearly Gates. It's a gamble you know, since God delights in sending people to Hell for the slightest infractions, but hey, it's your only out. So, bear your cross, you single, sorry, divorced thing you." (If you think I exaggerate you have never known a modern Pharisee. Consider yourself blessed.)

In a practical sense, I have known a number of people, who, were the innocent (non-cheating) parties to their respective marriages who, later in life, found each other and seemingly have formed very good marriages. They win souls to God. Have great joy in their salvation. What can I say?

Solid, Biblical families are the bedrock of the nation. The humanists are wrong. Man is not a higher form of animal that mates on pure instinct like a rabbit. Man and his chosen bride are to form a solid and enduring unit that shall not only procreate, but also hand down to each successive generation the knowledge and fear of God and his Law. In this way a nation grows, prospers, and has strength.

This process to be successful must be without the virus of infidelity. Nothing so disrupts the community of a nation like sexual deviation, promiscuity, fornication, adultery, and of course homosexuality. Jesus said, "Moses, for the hardness of your hearts, provided for a writ of divorce, but from the beginning it was not so." No doubt, in God's perfect view, a marriage between one man and one woman would never cease, except for death.

But this is not a perfect world. More and more we Christians find ourselves grappling with situations that force us to deal with gray areas, new territories, and heretofore unexplored exceptions to the rules, hoping that the Lord will find the decisions we make to be within his grace.

The Sabbath is clearly Saturday. Why do you insist that it is Sunday? I thought you believed in the Bible?

Why do you insist on putting words in my mouth? Who told you I insist that the Sabbath is Sunday? The Bible speaks of a number of Sabbaths. One Sabbath is the 7th day of the week. Sabbath days are calculated and re-calculated based on the phases of the moon and not our modern-day calendar. It is impossible to identify a single reoccurring day, such as Saturday, call it the Sabbath and have it mathematically come out on the 7th day, each and every week. Our Gregorian calendar is off by ¼ of a day per year, that is why you have a "leap year" every four years.

The very word "Saturday" appears nowhere in scripture. The

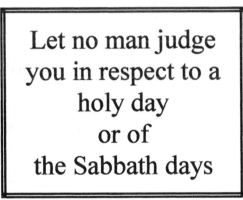

Let no man judge you in respect to a holy day or of the Sabbath days

giving of heathen names to the days of the week occurred much later than Old Testament scripture and was the work of the Romans. Saturn, the name of the god of agriculture, becomes Saturday, Moon day becomes Monday etc. Prior to Roman creativity, identifying the days of the week was for the most part numeric. Search your scriptures. The days of the week are numbered not named.

Paul specifically addressed Sabbath keeping in Romans 14:5 This scripture appears within a series of matters Paul had to address because, even in his day, there were "spiritual know it alls" who just couldn't live their lives, unless everyone else conformed their thinking and saw things their way. Paul said, "One man esteems one day above another, (Sabbath) one man esteems every day alike." Paul said, if they do it to honor the Lord (either way) it is good.

But let every man be fully persuaded in his own mind. See also Matthew 12, where the Lord deals with the practical matters of Sabbath. Notice how often in scripture, contentious issues such as Sabbath observation arise and are accompanied with the phrase "….. that they might have cause to accuse him."

Please don't allow yourself to fall into the trap of framing religious arguments, solely for the purpose of setting someone up to look bad, in order to make yourself look good. Whatever you desire to do with your life in regards to glorifying God, just do it and have pleasure and satisfaction in doing it and never mind what anyone else is doing or not doing. Believe me, your overall life will be enhanced by such an approach.

Further, Paul in Colossians 2:16 said, **"let no man judge you in respect to a holy day or of the Sabbath days:"** You wouldn't want to make an issue out of something Paul already addressed in scripture as a non-issue. Would you?

Does the Bible say anything about tattoos or body piercing? I want to do it but I'm not sure.

The fact that you say you are not sure, suggests to me that you have some mental reservations about proceeding. Do you feel peer pressure to do this? Is this one of those situations where "everyone else has one and I want to be like everyone else?" You might consider the admonition in Romans 12: 1-2.

"Present you bodies a living sacrifice, holy, acceptable unto God which is your reasonable service <u>and be ye not conformed to this world,</u> but be ye transformed by the renewing of your mind."

Just because "everybody else" is doing something, is not a sound

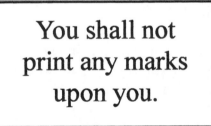

You shall not print any marks upon you.

basis upon which to make a decision about anything. Ask anyone over forty if they agree with me on that statement.

Scripture is clear and unambiguous in Leviticus 19:8 "Ye shall <u>not</u> make any cuttings in your flesh for the dead, nor print any marks upon you: I am the Lord."

Would you agree that a tattoo is a printing of a mark upon you?

I am amazed at the flood of interest in tattooing today. Years ago it seemed that only sailors or others who traveled abroad in the military were likely to get tattoos. Tattooing has historically been associated with alien and rather unenlightened cultures. But, today, because so much foreign influence from non-Christian countries has invaded our shores, I suppose it really should come as no surprise to anyone, that this heathen custom is gaining popularity in "Post-Christian" America.

Psychologists claim that low self-esteem is connected with tattooing and self-mutilation. Many young people today suffer from low self-esteem and poor self-image, so, I suppose they are in some ways almost predisposed to this type of thing.

Besides the Biblical prohibition, you really should consider the chance of infectious disease from the needle piercing, and the long- term toxic effect of ink permeating your soft tissue and adversely affecting your body's auto immune defenses. I really believe tattooing lowers your general health long-term. Remember God said, "Ye shall not... print any marks upon you." Listen to him.

Before you get your tattoo, I would strongly suggest you talk to people who are paying big money trying to remove the "Marks" of their youthful indiscretions. Tattoos are easy to get, but almost

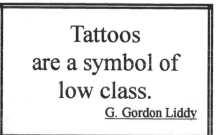

Tattoos
are a symbol of
low class.
G. Gordon Liddy

impossible to get rid of. After a little time, they fade and get that sick purple look and you are stuck with it. Not to mention, you might ask some of the guys, what it is like to have an old girlfriend's name, that is no longer at his side, permanently imbedded in his skin. That must be a real bummer.

G. Gordon Liddy, an attorney, former Nixon appointee, former FBI agent and now a national radio talk show host, had a good response to a young woman caller who asked him what he thought about tattoos.

Liddy said, that in the professional world tattoos are regarded as a sign of low-class. Regardless of what movie star has one (who said movie stars were any particular class anyway). He related the story of how, a young woman, for whatever reason, got a tattoo on her leg. Years later she met a very successful man whom she felt was quite a nice catch, and potential husband. He invited her to meet his parents at their lake property. Everything seemed fine, until she donned her bathing suit and it was apparent she had a tattoo.

You may think these people were very narrow, but the sight of the tattoo sent a message that this woman was not of appropriate breeding for their family.   People who have high regard for themselves, the future of their families and fortunes sometimes can balk at what might appear to you or I to be a small matter.

I think Liddy hit it on the head. Tattoos are a symbol of low class.   God's people are high class. Things we do, matter to people and to God. The choices we make affect us.

Your body is called the temple of the Holy Ghost. Please do not defile your temple. (I Corinthian 3:17)   I think if you consult the scriptures above, and give consideration to what your responsibility may be for the care and keeping of God's temple, (your body) you will probably ask the Lord to deliver you from this present temptation.

Why should I give tithes and offerings to a man, when I can give directly to the poor and other causes just the same? I get so sick of hearing preachers asking for money all the time.

You think you're sick of hearing it, I'm sick of asking all the time.

Plus, I'm sick of hearing the grocer telling me how much I owe him, and the property tax man saying pay up or get out. Not to mention, I'm sick of the insurance company demanding their due, and then there's the kids tuition for supposed education, and car payments, and .... on it goes.

I notice that if the preacher isn't asking your support of the Kingdom of God, the football stadium is collecting tithes and offerings at the gate. So is the World Wrestling Federation and the stage and theatre, the bowling alley asks for your support, as do all restaurants, gymnasiums and health clubs, hair salons and barber shops, beer joints and nightclubs, motels and cruise liners, vacation getaways from Disney World to Cancun all seem to feel that what they offer is worth giving to and supporting.

If that isn't bad enough, go to your mailbox and in it you will find a myriad of foundations doing good things, like

> # Where your treasure is, there will your heart be also.

allegedly finding cures for diseases, and guess what? They need your support.

But, what really galls me, are the perverts from the American Civil Liberties Union who want to sue Christians, Churches and Christian organizations. These extremist hate groups like the

Southern Poverty Law Center, and the Anti-defamation League of B'nai Brith get millions in individual support and large grants from corporate generosity. You may not be aware of this, but there are organized sodomites who want special rights and do they ever raise the millions for their causes. It's amazing to me, how the "unholy" will reach into their pockets and give support to what they believe in. Just let some no-morals rock star sing on a TV tele-thon and watch the million$$$$ come rolling in.

The truth of the matter is, this is a world in which you pay and pay and pay. In this life, everything that has value, and one way or the other, it is measured in dollars. Matthew 6:21 "Where your treasure is, there will your heart be also." Where is your heart?

Forgive me, I guess I kind of went on and on. I think your question was, why should you give to a man, when you could just give your tithes and offerings directly to the poor etc. The simple answer is you could. If, that was what tithing and giving to the Church was all about. But, it is not.

Tithing is a payment on a unilateral, contractual agreement, between you and God. Tithe is brought into the storehouse where the grain is kept according to Malachi 3:7-12 Tithing is a command that believers since Abraham delight in complying with and scorners delight in stumbling at. I am amazed at how some people think that 10% is a lot of money to contribute to their church.

If a store advertised a 10% off sale, their customers wouldn't give it the time of day, because 10% is nothing. People won't walk across the street to save 10%. That's why I personally think God chose the tithe. It's really nothing. Just 10%. Before I was a Christian, I supported the devil with a lot more than 10% of what I had coming in and the devil was not in a position to bless me. Rather he cursed me. What a rip-off ! God's tithe is a bargain.

Let me ask you something. You say you want to give to the poor directly? Tally up your income for the year, check your balance sheet and see if 10% (the tithe) of that amount went directly to anyone in need. If anything near 10% did, you would be the only person I know who does that, outside of systematic givers who practice a tithing covenant with their God and their local Body of Christ.

I don't mean to be offensive, but it was Judas who complained about "all the waste and mismanagement," as a woman worshipped the Lord pouring an alabaster box of precious ointment on Jesus' feet. It was Judas who said, "instead of dumping this out on the feet of the Lord, it might better have been sold and given to the poor." The Bible reveals why he said this,

> # Give
> ## and it shall be
> ## given unto you.

"...not that he cared for the poor, but because he carried the money and was a thief. " (John 12:6)

It was the money critic that ultimately betrayed the Lord. Please don't be a person who talks like Judas. I have heard the "give to the poor rather than to a man or the Church" argument many times before. I'm sorry. It is an old and hollow argument.

The Lord loves a cheerful giver. If you have received something from the Lord, then cheerfully give. Jesus said in Luke 6:38,

"Give, and it shall be given unto you; good measure, pressed down, and shaken together, and running over shall men give into your bosom, For with the same measure that you give it out, it shall be measured back to you again."

You can't out give the Lord. The Lord had this to say specifically about unbelievers who did not tithe..

Malachi Chapter 3: 7-10 paraphrased

"You people are no different than your parents. My commandments mean nothing to you." The Lord says, "return unto me, and I will return unto you ." But you say, "How shall we return to you?" God replies, "Will a man rob God? Yet ye have robbed me you pack of thieves" But you say, "How have we robbed you?" God says, " In tithes and offerings. And because of this you are cursed with a curse for you and this whole nation have robbed me. Bring all the tithes into the storehouse, that there may be food in my house. And don't just take my word for it, test me and see, if I will not open you windows of heaven, and pour you out a blessing, that there shall not be room enough to receive it." .

Are you blessed or cursed? The power is in your hands. You decide. Read Malachi 3 in your Bible and I think you'll agree that God is making you an offer you can't ignore.

I have a friend who won't eat pork or shrimp. He says it's against God's law and I say that the law was done away with at the cross. What do you say?

Why do Americans insist on eating so much junk that is hard to digest, clogs up the arteries, gets hung up in their bowels, then rots and putrefies forming cancers that have to be surgically removed and otherwise ruins their health? I agree with your friend. God's law says the swine and shell fish you refer to, are "unclean." Unclean as used in reference to swine and certain fish, means *unhealthy.*

Does it seem reasonable to you that God would be double-minded? That something could become healthy today, that God declared thousands of years ago was not healthy?

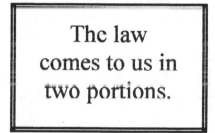

The law comes to us in two portions.

This is not a heaven or hell issue, but I'm convinced it does have a bearing on how fast you get there. In 3 John 1:2 the writer wishes that, "above all things you may prosper and be in health." God really only wants what's best for us and your having good health is important to him.

Leviticus 11:7 -11 " The swine...he is unclean to you,... of their flesh shall ye not eat, and their carcass shall you not touch, they are unclean to you. And of fish, all that have not fins and scales in the seas, and in the rivers,....shall be abomination to you...you shall not eat of their flesh."

Maybe you're like me and what the Bible says is sufficient. If you need a second opinion, go to any health food store, or consult with most any life extension experts. They will tell you that from a metabolic and scientific standpoint, eating these creatures is not healthy for you. In fact, ask any of your friends who are seeing a heart specialist, "What was the first food item your doctor told you to avoid?" Clue - It was probably pork!

Americans are a sick bunch. Nearly a hundred countries of the world have life expectancies longer that we do. Do you think our consumption of swine and shell fish has anything to do with it?

Incredibly, it's the Christians and their leaders who are most responsible for misleading the entire nation on this matter of clean and unclean foods. Ask most of them and they'll tell you that what I have quoted above from Leviticus is Old Testament Law and doesn't apply to us today. But what they evidently fail to understand, is that the Law comes to us in two portions.

First there's the ceremonial law, which is what scripture calls a "schoolmaster to bring us to Christ," (Galatians 3:24) that Law ended at the cross. The other portion of Law is the code of statutes and ordinances, which provides the basis for modern civil and criminal common-law, and the health codes, referred to above. God has never repealed the health, civil or criminal codes.

Jesus said, "If you love me keep my commandments." (John 14:15)

"Think not that I am come to destroy the Law" (Matthew 5:17)

"Whosoever therefore shall break one of these least commandments, (like eating unclean foods) and shall teach men so, (it's done on a routine basis) he shall be called the least in the kingdom of heaven, but whosoever shall do and teach them, the same shall be called great in the kingdom of heaven." (Matthew 5:19) When you realize the full impact of this, it gets really scary.

I don't know how many times someone has given the following

answer to justify their lust for eating recycled trash like swine and shrimp. Its incredible but true. It goes like this.

Peter had a vision in Acts 10, wherein all these unclean creatures were offered to him on a sheet let down from heaven and the Lord himself told him to slay and eat. Peter said, "Not so Lord for nothing common or unclean has ever entered my mouth," but the Lord said, "Whatsoever I have cleansed that call not thou unclean."

Those who simply can't live without ham and bacon will often retort, "So there, God says you can eat pork."

Alright, if that was what God was trying to get across to Peter, why then, did Peter say,

"Of a truth, **I perceive that God is no respecter of persons**. But in every nation he that feareth him and worketh righteousness is accepted with him." (Acts 10:34)

The sheet of unclean beasts was *symbolic* of **people** that Peter up to this point considered **common and unclean!** God has often used symbolism in scripture. God used the dove symbolically to appear for the Holy Spirit. Do you think the spirit of the Lord is a bird? He referred to King Herrod as a fox. Did Herrod really have a tail? Get real.

God's purpose in Peter's rooftop visionary experience, had nothing to do with food. It had to do with Peter's momentary tribal prejudices against Gentiles. God just used the food vision to convey the concept. Do you honestly think the God of creation would make a top priority of promoting Ham and Swiss on Rye?

Here is what I really find amazing today. There is ample scriptural support to doctrinally mandate that Christians observe God's food laws; even if only for their health sake. However, good people, in otherwise very conservative circles, choose to ignore, and in some cases, they even belittle God's law on health. Why is it, that we Christians have such a natural tendency towards self-destruction?

If God calls the consumption of pork and shell fish "abomination," how can anyone consider polluting God's temple (your body being the temple of God) with abominable, unhealthy, heart-stopping, artery-clogging, foods; to be a non-issue? I must confess, I find that type of thinking to be incomprehensible.

Nearly every time I visit a holiness church function and food is served, invariably, there is "Ole Miss Piggy," proudly presented for consumption. I don't get it. When the scripture is so clear, why do God's people insist on being so obstinate?

If there is something about this whole contradiction, that I am missing or if you can help me understand this better, please tell me. I am open to your insights.

Proverbs 4:7   "Wisdom is the principal thing;   therefore get wisdom; and with all they getting get understanding."

A Christian friend of mine insists that it Is a sin for women to cut their hair. Where is that In the Bible?

Your friend is probably referring to I Corinthians 11:6 - 15 where it says in part, "...if it be a shame for a woman to be shorn or shaven, let her be covered." and "..if a woman have long hair, it is a glory to her; for her hair is given her for a covering."

This is an interesting subject. It has also been a great source of unnecessary contention and confusion amongst some Christians for years. I hope my answer does not serve to simply increase the confusion and contention.

I recently had a well-meaning pastor tell me that this doctrine, of prohibiting women from cutting their hair, was a Heaven or Hell, foundational doctrine. It may be a *tradition,* deeply rooted in a number of what are called, fundamentalist, conservative or holiness churches, but, to claim that it is foundational, or has any eternal significance, is simply unsupportable.

If it were a Heaven or Hell issue, wouldn't there be more than one discussion?

There are a number of foundational doctrines in scripture that form the bedrock of the Christian faith and are of eternal significance, but this isn't one of them. The following discussion provides the main reason why it is not.

The Bible has a standard for the admissibility of "allegation evidence" in a criminal trial and I believe the rationale for that standard, is an applicable test for any doctrine that claims to be more than a custom or tradition. The Biblical, minimum legal standard, for the admissibility of a trespass allegation, is that the allegation must be supported from the mouths of two, or preferably, three separate and independent sources. (Matthew 18:16) A trespass is a low-level criminal act sometimes resulting in a damage. Further,

"...at the mouth of *two witnesses, or three witnesses*, shall he that is worthy of death be put to death; but at the mouth of <u>one witness he shall not be put to death</u>," (Deut. 17:6)

One witness's testimony, is insufficient grounds to support either a minor or a serious accusation in Biblical law. It is important to note, that I Corinthians 11, is the <u>only place in scripture </u>where a "hair" discussion of this kind appears. If, it were a Heaven or Hell issue, wouldn't there be more than one discussion?

This is a free country. Every person has an inalienable right to "freely exercise" their religious beliefs. Any person, who desires to incorporate this (or any other) hair tradition into their own personal walk, simply because they have a preference or desire to do so, could certainly be justified in doing it. However, an honest analysis of scripture will show that there is insufficient, supplemental scriptural support, to maintain a more significant, Heaven or Hell, doctrinal statement.

If a woman desires to live her entire life, and never cut her hair - Hallelujah! Do it to the Glory of God! But, do it for that reason only.

Remember, my preacher friend maintained (as some do) that this was a Heaven or Hell issue. If that is his position, then that doctrinal point, (in my mind) should be held to the same Biblical evidence test as the one God insists be applied to an order for execution. The thought being, that upon the execution of the sentence of death, the recipient will be on their way to Heaven or

Hell, one way or the other. God evidently feels, that on very serious matters, nothing of consequence should move forward, that is not well established in law, and supported with evidence, that is clear and convincing.

The Bible provides <u>dozens</u> of scriptural evidences to support baptism in Jesus Name, the deity of Christ, the Holy Ghost baptism being evidenced by speaking in tongues, and the lordship of Christ over his Church as *foundational*

> # The no cutting issue has been a tradition.
>
> # <u>Not a bad tradition mind you</u>
> # But a tradition just the same.

doctrines upon which the Church is established. The doctrinal matters I just delineated above, are widely recognized foundations, supported with voluminous scriptural authority and not mere *traditions* of men, imposed in this case, only upon women, based upon one, rather vague, scriptural citation.

All of the widely established and irrefutable Christian doctrines, are clearly and concisely found within our Lord's Word, but, what a woman is to do or not do with her hair, is not even hinted at elsewhere in scripture. Those who love to be contentious about this and other points, unfortunately, tend to end up in the camp of those who strain at gnats and swallow camels.

Imagine for just a moment, that you and I have just been transported in a time machine, back to Christ' day. Jesus has just performed a miracle in opening a man's blind eyes. How would you feel if you over-heard a Pharisee's objection, that the miracle had violated the Sabbath, or, what if we heard a complaint being

made that Jesus' disciples were eating with unwashed hands.....
Would that seem bizarre?   But, that's exactly what happened
back then.   Incredibly, 2000 years later, we're still dealing with
the same, narrow, misdirected thinking and conduct involving
many matters.

It's too easy to get sidetracked with argumentative tangents,
regarding the "minors," while the "majors" end up undone. I have
seen good people, quite literally, obsess over this, and other doctrinal points. It is sad.   The entire world, is dead in trespasses and sins, and they desperately need to be reached with what is truly necessary   and eternally life-saving.

> # Be careful (in going overboard with outward holiness) that you do not find yourself minimizing the true sacrifice for sin that no man can duplicate.

The first century Church was established, without a printing press, without a
written New Testament, and with no mention of women's hair in
any apostolic preaching. The Church was over forty years old by
the time I Corinthians was written, and nearly 1500 years passed
before Gutenberg's printing press began to publish it in any
numerical way.

"...it seemed good to the Holy Ghost, and to us, to lay upon you
no greater burden than these *necessary things*, that you abstain
from meats offered to idols, and from blood, and from things
strangled, and from fornication, from which if you keep
yourselves, you shall do well." (Acts 15:28, 29)

Do the <u>necessary things </u>and you shall do well! Do you find it interesting that of the four things mentioned by the Apostle as *necessary*, three of them were related to food, and not one about hair?

Even, if I Corinthians 11, was referring to a complete prohibition against women cutting their hair, it appears only once, without further independent support and furthermore, it is directed specifically to the Corinthian Church. The reference, no doubt, meant something to Paul and perhaps to a specific cultural observance at that time, in that place; but, to apply it to Christian women today as a hard and fast, Heaven or Hell issue is simply not fair, is doctrinally insufficient and logically unsupportable.

> The really dangerous aspect in all this tradition/doctrinal confusion is the tendency for a mindset to develop that can place so-called personal holiness, in direct competition to the cross

Believe me, I know something about the "no-cutting issue." I taught it for years without seriously considering why and then when I did study it, it was apparent that the teaching was clearly not a doctrinal mandate and that it was only a tradition and nothing more. Not a bad tradition, mind you, but a tradition just the same.

We at the Adrian Church, observe some traditions of our own, that are not doctrinally significant. Perhaps you do also. That's fine, so long as you are cognizant of the difference between traditions and doctrines. Both are good when kept in their proper venues.

Having said all that, let me point out that included in I Corinthians 11, is the mention (Nazerite vows notwithstanding) that it is a shame for a man to have long hair, but that it is a glory for the woman to have long hair. In this world of aggressive homo-sexualization of society, the making of a clear distinction between the sexes by hair style and length, makes very good and Biblically supportable sense. In fact, as far as I have been able to discover, virtually all advanced civilizations, for thousands of years, have made the distinction in the sexes clearly apparent by the wearing of gender-distinctive hair styles, generally along the lines of long hair on women, and shorter hair on men.

> If you are not careful, a delusional attitude can develop that convinces you that salvation is accomplished by Christ' atoning blood, *plus* your individual lifestyle and daily sacrificial "holy" living

But, a woman having long hair, is not to be confused with a doctrine that puts a strict prohibition on cutting. The two matters are clearly distinct. A woman's hair can be trimmed and healthy, and still be culturally recognizable as being long and feminine as opposed to being short and masculine, like her male counter-part.

It is pretty common-place among the lesbian community, for a woman to have a "butch' haircut if she radically resents the male and sexually desires to take his place in her lifestyle role. So, we see culturally, a woman having her hair styled like a man's, could definitely send the wrong signal to those around her and thus, at the same time, be offensive to the Holy Spirit.

If the position taken by a particular church or individual, is that a Christian woman's hair should be long, and the man's hair cut, and thus not long; that position, I believe, can be supported with significant circumstantial evidence, and cultural sensibility. However, to make the mere cutting or trimming of a woman's hair a sinful act, in and of itself, is a complete stretch of what the scripture teaches and is error.

History shows that in Biblical times and to some degree in modern times as well, that if a woman was caught in the act of adultery, in lieu of being decapitated (adultery being an executable offense) her hair was simply shaved off. Evidently, the theory was, that symbolically cutting the hair, was close enough to cutting the throat. In this way, if her hair was shaved off, the offending woman bore the shame of her act if she went out in public. Thus, I Corinthians 11:6 "..if it be a *shame for a woman to be shorn or shaven,*" makes complete sense.

The shame was not in trimming her hair. The shame was being caught in sexual immorality and being publicly humiliated for having dishonored her head (the man is her head.)

The whole "hair" discussion in I Corinthians is about the Lordship of Christ. A woman demonstrates her respect for God's order by respecting her head (the head of the woman is the man.) She has long hair. The man demonstrates his worship and submission to God's order of authority by not having long hair. It's as simple as that.

The really dangerous aspect in all this tradition/doctrinal confusion is the tendency for a mindset to develop that can place so-called personal holiness, in direct competition to the cross. We are saved by the grace of God and the shed blood of Jesus, plus nothing. There is no way to improve on Jesus' death on the cross for our sins. But, if you are not careful, a delusional attitude can develop that convinces you that salvation is accomplished by Christ' atoning blood, *plus* your individual lifestyle and daily sacrificial "holy" living.

I warn you. If you think for one minute that you can make yourself more attractive to the Lord through any efforts intended to make your physical appearance extra-holy and spiritually significant, (with or without your hair) be careful, that you do not at the same time minimize the true sacrifice for sin that no man can duplicate. I fear, that there will be people at the judgment, that are going to find out too late, that what they were told was holiness and a high standard, was, in reality, nothing more than a modern-day version of pharisaical self-righteousness.

Here's my personal view. Understand - I'm not a woman. But, if I was I would have long hair. How long? Certainly longer than my male counter-parts. I would try to keep it as healthy and clean as possible, so as to bring glory to Christ and not bring attention to myself. But, my decision would be based primarily on culture and scriptures supplemental to I Corinthians 11, but not excluding it.

As a man, I believe the scripture and my culture teaches that my hair should not be long or effeminate. A true believer's hair, dress and general appearance should always be with the intent to be modest, not extravagant and always presented in such a way, so as to bring glory to God's order of headship.

As a side note: There is a curious mention at I Corinthians 11:10,

"...for this cause ought the women to have power on their heads, because of the angels."

Some, unintended fictional accounts, have been published, speculating what is meant by the above cited verse. One, such, published speculation, invents a bizarre and almost idolatrous view of women's hair, and the power a woman possesses by virtue of the fact, that she does not cut it (a kind of Samson syndrome - gender inversed.) This particular book implies that women, virtually control their life's destiny and even the future of God's Kingdom, based on what they do with their hair. All such writings I am familiar with on that particular, "power on their heads" question, are nothing more than speculation, conjecture and mostly fiction presented as fact. A truly scary proposition.

While I personally enjoy, a certain amount of intellectual speculation, reading between the lines and "thinking out loud," about a lot of things; there is no way to know for certain what this comment by Paul meant, either in his day, or what bearing it might possibly have for our's. We see through a glass darkly. (I Corinthians 13:12)

Deuteronomy 22:5 says " The woman shall not wear that which pertains unto a man, neither shall a man put on a woman's garment; for all that do so are abomination unto the Lord thy God. If a woman wears pants, isn't that sin?

Here we go again. This question brings into one intersection a fascinating traffic jam of thinking,

While it is not clear what is meant by "pertaining to a man" or this scripture's relevance to us today. I am very sure about the meaning of the phrase "all that do so are abomination unto the Lord thy God."

Abominations are things, or acts that God finds extremely detestable, filthy, revolting and unacceptable. The Bible declares many things to be abominable. (including eating pork) Among them are certain sexual matters. Leviticus 18:22 pronounces sexual relations with those of the same sex to be abomination. This should come as no surprise. God destroyed Sodom and Gomorrah because of its wickedness and homosexual obsession. Anything that crosses over the clear

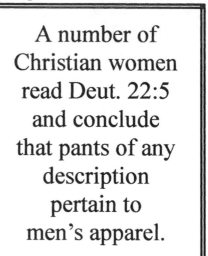

A number of Christian women read Deut. 22:5 and conclude that pants of any description pertain to men's apparel.

distinction between male and female is taboo with God. God condemns male effeminacy declaring in I Corinthians 6:9 that the "effeminate, and abusers of themselves with mankind shall not inherit the Kingdom of God."

I am persuaded that Duet. 22:5 quoted above, is directed to those who cross-dress with the intention of indulging in forbidden and abominable homosexual conduct. I am furthermore convinced that most women who wear jeans or slacks have no ulterior homosexual motives.

However, I am equally persuaded that there are some women (and men) who enjoy wearing tight and revealing jeans or slacks for the sole purpose of attracting the attention of the opposite sex. I wish to point out, that while this may be a violation of Deut. 22:5, I am sure it is a violation of a myriad of other scriptures dealing with adultery, lust, immodesty, lasciviousness, licentiousness, the spirit of the harlot, and the like.

I have known a good number of outstanding Christian women who would rather be hit by a Mac Truck than ever wear or be seen in a pair of slacks or jeans. With most of these women, their desire to wear dresses as opposed to pants, is born of their individual interpretation of scripture, together with their personal dedication and desire to walk in a high standard with their Lord. They read Deut. 22:5 and conclude that pants of any description "pertain" to men's apparel.

I have also known a significant number of equally dedicated and wonderful, God-fearing women, who simply don't want to be miserable when they go out in blistering, blowing, cold, winter weather, or for whatever practical work reason, occasionally wear slacks or loose fitting jeans (I emphasize loose fitting, you don't have to be a genius to know why that makes a difference.) The latter often wear an additional jacket or covering for a completely modest appearance.

I remember seeing a special television program, all about baboons one time on the Animal Kingdom Channel. When the female baboon is ready to mate, she bends all the way over and grabs her heels and in this way exposes her genitals to the male baboons. In time, one of the males runs over and begins beating on her back with his fists, then runs off to the bush. If the female chooses, she then makes another approach to the male and they eventually mate. I think I got a revelation from God that day.

I don't know what the beating on the back by the male baboon was all about, but the exposing of the genitals was obvious. Isn't that what some women (and some men) who lower themselves to a beastly mentality do, when they wear skin tight slacks or jeans? Do they intend to expose themselves and get attention from the opposite sex?

I have respect for both groups of Christian women - those who wear dresses only and those who at times wear modest slacks or jeans. Although both groups

> God's dress standard for both sexes has always been modesty.

hold differing views, I have found their heart's attitude toward God, is generally the same.

I also respect any church congregation that wishes to abide by an agreed upon standard of separation and strive for consistency in dress or standards of attire. If that means, pants are for men and dresses are for women, so be it.

The police have a uniform. So do the military, and the medical profession. What is wrong with Christians having a distinctive way of dress that is clearly modest and set apart from the rest of society. Romans 12:1 instructs us, "Present your bodies a living sacrifice, holy, acceptable unto God, which is your reasonable service. And be not conformed to the world." II Corinthians 6:17 "...come out from among them (the unbelievers who live in spiritual darkness) and be ye separate."

I am not a woman but I have been asked, if I was what would I wear?

I would dress in whatever I felt would celebrate my God-given femininity and at the same time would be appropriate for each given situation. Incidentally, I have ugly knees and I have no doubt that I would keep them covered up, probably with a skirt or dress.

Short skirts and high-cut slits would be out. I wouldn't want to get to the final, eternal judgment and find out I had been a contributor to someone's sin, because my choice in clothing encouraged lusting after my body.

I'm not saying that I would never wear pants. But speaking for myself, I really think if celebrating God-given femininity is the desired objective, I would lean heavily toward modest dresses and skirts. I just find dresses to be more feminine. The last comment is not doctrinal, its simply a preference. However, let me quickly state that my conclusions are largely based on culture and scriptures supplemental to Deuteronomy 22:5

But let's be real. I'm not a woman, so I don't have to be concerned, do I?

Paul said, "Let every man (and woman) be fully persuaded......" Whatever you decide to do with your life and lifestyle, just be sure to ask that still small voice within, and then proceed in the best possible way to live your life so as to bring glory to God and harmony within the Body of Christ.

God's dress standard for both sexes has always been modesty. See I Timothy 2:9. If a dress, or any other covering is enticing, revealing, skin-tight etc., it violates God's law on modesty and that is as serious a transgression as cross-dressing, in my view.

Finally, let's see what God says the best-dressed Christians should wear. It's in Ephesians 6:14-17.

"Stand therefore having your loins girt about with truth, and having on the breastplate of righteousness and you feet shod with the preparation of the gospel of peace. Above all taking the shield of faith, wherewith ye shall be able to quench all the fiery darts of the wicked. And take the helmet of salvation and the sword of the spirit which is the word of God."

I know that Jesus never drank wine. Why then did Paul say in I Timothy 5:23 to "take a little wine for your stomach's sake?" It seems so contradictory.

How do you know Jesus never drank wine? If he did, what difference would it make? He turned water into wine at the marriage celebration. (John 2) It was his first miracle. Do you think he made Welch's Grape Juice? The governor of the feast said it was unusually good wine. The use of wine was obviously widespread and common in Bible lands and in all of Europe, not only in Jesus day, but up to the present. Consider Jesus own words from Matthew 11:18-19

"For John came neither eating nor drinking, and they say, He hath a devil. The Son of man came eating and *drinking* and they say, Behold a man gluttonous, and a *winebibber*....."

Why else would Jesus be called a winebibber if he had no association or contact with wine?

Clever preachers will try to weasel their way around the obvious and explain that this does not in anyway prove that Jesus consumed wine. I say, what's the point? If Jesus drank and manufactured wine, it certainly doesn't take anything away from his holiness or divinity in my mind. In fact, it makes him that much more real to me. Having a savior that drank wine with his meals, doesn't bother me.

> # Do I think that making such an admission in writing is dangerous? You bet I do!
>
> (This whole book is dangerous to my health)

I do find bothersome however, religious pinheads who for silly,

77

usually self-serving reasons, insist on inventing arguments and spurious definitions from the Greek and Hebrew to support a position that Jesus somehow did not do, what he obviously did.

When you begin your question with, "I know that Jesus never drank wine..." you exhibit evidence of either, denominational indoctrination, willing ignorance or simply a lack of intellectual enlightenment. I encourage you to join the ranks of those who are developing their ability to think and accept the Bible and Christ' teachings at face value and reject all teachings which are illogical or fraudulent.

> "Ya know
> Brother Strawcutter,
> There's some things I really
> wish Paul hadn't said"

On the matter of a "little wine for your stomach's sake..." The reference is, no doubt, medicinal. Inspect the label on your bottle of Nyquil. It's 25% alcohol. Do you ever take such medications for your stomach's sake? I have friends from the old country who are outstanding Christians who occasionally have wine with their meals. They're never drunk and in fact they view people who abuse wine and other beverages to excess as disgraceful. You could transport them back to Jesus time and they would probably fit right in.

When a denomination takes a position that says the consumption of any alcoholic beverage is a sin, they're faced with a problem. They must invent an airtight teaching that also says that Jesus did not consume wine, or else they would find themselves in the position of saying Jesus sinned, if he in fact drank wine.

I can fully appreciate anyone's desire to discourage the use and abuse of any substance that has an established history of adverse and negative implications like alcohol. I don't want my generation, or my grandchildren's generation to rot their livers out with booze, or addict themselves with cocaine, or food, or sex, or anything else. But, I just cannot bring myself to engage in a dishonest presentation and twisting of scripture to try to reach those ends.

Do I believe Jesus drank wine? Yes. Do I believe I Timothy 5:23 suggests a little wine for health and medicinal reasons when necessary? Yes. Do I think that making such an admission in writing is dangerous? You bet I do!

I believe it is dangerous because it's possible some weak person looking for an excuse to get blasted, may choose to do so. If someone reads this and they become an alcoholic they may say, "Pastor Strawcutter said it was alright, so he's to blame for my sorry state."

I run the risk of attacks by the official critics. Other preachers. Its always dangerous to open your mouth and risk losing friends and associates. Nobody likes criticism or the feeling of being condemned for taking a politically incorrect position. Not even me.

I remember talking to a dear old friend and Bible teacher, Marvin Arnold, years ago about this subject. I said, " What about what Paul said here in I Timothy 5:23, taking a little wine for thy stomach's sake?" After a few moments of painful reflection he replied, "Ya know Brother Strawcutter, there's some things, I really wish Paul hadn't said."

Well, my friend may wish Paul hadn't said it, but he did and it's there. Another fellow minister when questioned about this subject simply said, he really didn't know what Paul meant by the statement. I can respect both answers.

My personal advice is, don't drink at all.

The Italians say red wine reduces cholesterol and to back up their claim, they statistically do have very little heart disease, but we're Americans, and we Americans tend to go to excess in everything. That's why we have so many alcoholics with diseased livers. And, let us not fail to mention, that as a nation, we constitute some of the fattest most wasteful people on earth. Many of us, just don't know when to stop. So, why get started?

Most preachers take the zero tolerance position they do, because they know very well, that the average person would never "take a *little* wine" for their stomach's sake. They probably feel like its better to preach a little falsehood, perpetuate a bit of myth and have less drunks to deal with. Who knows. Maybe they're right and I'm wrong.

Romans 13 tells us to obey all the laws of the government. If the Federal Communications Commission says you need a license to be on the radio, then why does Pastor Strawcutter violate Romans 13 by transmitting his illegal radio station on 99.3 fm?

This is a great question. Entire books have been written on Romans 13 and submission to the civil magistrate. Let's talk a little bit about government.

The first and ultimate best government is self-government. If every individual did unto others, as they would have them do unto themselves, you would have no need of jails, courts, police and etc. Unfortunately, there are people among us who lack the internal self-regulation needed to keep them within reasonable lawful boundaries. For them, the law of the civil magistrate outlined in Romans 13 applies.

> Governmental powers inconsistent with God's law have no eternal force, effect or legitimacy

You have summarized one of the great misconceptions of this portion of Romans when you claim that it, "tells us to obey all the laws of the government." Who told you that? That is not at all, what Romans 13 says. Unquestioning, and slavish compliance to everything that some government agency dictates, cannot be what is implied by Romans 13. If it was, then virtually all the Christian believers in the Bible including Paul, the writer of Romans, were in violation. Their religion was illegal. Paul was a lawyer and the writer of Romans. Why was he in jail most of his ministry? If he believed he had a God-given duty to bow down and respect every ordinance that the Roman government insisted upon, he must have been the biggest hypocrite in the Bible.

And let's not forget the Lord himself. Jesus incited a riot in the Temple Treasury, and when Peter and John were locked up in prison, the Lord perpetrated a jail break!

More modernly, the United States of America was founded upon a rebellion against the government and laws of Great Britain, yet, no other nation in recorded history has been as blessed as ours. Was it established in violation of Romans 13? Did God bless a rebellion?

> # Didn't Rosa Parks know it was against the law to ride on the front seat of the bus?

Rosa Parks is hailed as a wonderful person who evidently was also a Romans 13 violator and civil rights liberator. Didn't she know it was against the law to ride on the front seat of the bus?

Have you considered how Christian missionaries "smuggle" Bibles into communist countries like China, in violation of Chinese law, and afterward receive praises for perpetrating such crimes? But according to your view, all the government persecuted Christians in the Bible including John the Revelator, banished to the Isle of Patmos, "for the word of God and the testimony of Jesus," the Apostle Paul, writer of over one half the New Testament, plus others, like George Washington and the Founding Fathers and an innumerable host of other God-fearing people were all Romans 13 violators. If I understand the logic of your position, the people I just mentioned above, who by the way, suffered horribly for their particular acts of conscience, would have suffered no problems whatsoever, if they had simply obeyed the laws of their respective governments.

Romans 13: 1,2,5 in part says: " Let every soul be subject unto the higher powers. For there is no power but of God: the powers that be are ordained of God. Whosoever therefore resisteth the power, resisteth the ordinance of God."

> # The power to say where is the power to say nowhere

"The powers that be are ordained of God." (Romans 13:1)

For a better understanding of what Paul meant when he wrote Romans 13, try reading this verse as follows:
"The powers that *be legitimate* are ordained of God."

Any governmental powers that are inconsistent with God's law have no eternal force, effect or legitimacy at all.

Who really has the ultimate authority to declare what the Law is? (Clue: Its not anyone who must run for election.)

"There is one lawgiver….." (James 4:12)

In this nation, when you have a legal dispute, you can appeal to several legal layers and ultimately end up at the U.S. Supreme Court. After you get to that level, you have run out of appeals. But wait, there is one more Judge - God himself. And wouldn't you agree, that history has established his opinion, is really the only one that counts?

On the matter of the FCC and my radio station, have you considered that the air was created by God, before there was any government anywhere? Furthermore, current FCC guidelines have the effect of suppressing God-given, free speech and free exercise rights of religion guaranteed by the First Amendment.

I am quite familiar with the FCC. I became an amateur radio operator at the age of fourteen, and have a background in law in addition to my Biblical studies. I have prayerfully proceeded with counsel on every matter related to the exercise in freedom, that we in Adrian call Radio Free Lenawee 99.3 FM. The radio station I founded in 1996, has the distinction of being the longest running so-called "pirate" radio station of its size in U.S. history.

Any number of things have happened over the past five years that indicate to me that God has been with us. When the Federal Government sued me the first time, in 1997, the circumstances were so incredibly in my favor that even my professed atheist attorney exclaimed, "Strawcutter, you must have a god that looks out for you favorably."

If God is favorable to me and my radio station, then is the Lord himself a Romans 13 violator?

I give thanks to the Lord for all the families that have been added to the Body of Christ as a result of our radio outreach. Only eternity will reveal the total impact that broadcasting our worship services live, has had on people. Across the radio airwaves, all over Lenawee County came the sounds of tongues and prophetic interpretations, testimonials of miracles, great choir singing and the glorious sounds of hundreds of people praising God! The evening air space over Adrian has even been filled with the melodic voice of Alexander Scourby, reading the scriptures, providing for many people who have never read the Bible, the opportunity to hear the entire Bible read to them flawlessly from Genesis through Revelation. If I'm a criminal for doing that without the blessing of the Federal Government, then so be it.

Some people ask, "Why don't you just get an FCC license?" As if it were that easy.

It has been said that, "The power to say where, is the power to say nowhere." This is certainly true when it comes to starting a radio station. If you have ever built a house, you know something about the frustration of dealing with bureaucratic power. If you think building inspectors are unreasonable, just try dealing with any agency of the Federal Government and you can multiply your frustration level by ten!

> I discovered that the only people pushing the FCC to get us off the air were the owners of a local station that features Country Western music.
>
> ———
>
> That's it.

In this country, greedy corporate powers rule. If you saw the movie "Wag the Dog," with Dustin Hoffman, you will understand what I mean when I tell you that the corporate radio industry, "wags" the FCC, and not the other way around. There are huge and powerful corporations like Jaycor and Clear Channel to name just two, that together own over one thousand radio stations! (and they call me a pirate???) They have an agenda, and believe me, it is not spreading truth and liberty throughout the land. It is clear, that the goal of the corporate pirates is to gain monopolistic control of everything that is heard, thought about, and merchandized in this country.

One guy asked, "What if, what's on the news is not true?" His friend replied, "What would it matter, if we all believe the same lies."

Jeremiah 5:31 "The prophets prophesy falsely, ...and <u>my people love to have it so</u>; and what will you do in the end?"

Incidentally, Isaiah 5:8 pronounces judgment against monopolies like radio giants Jaycor and Clear Channel.

"Woe unto them that join house to house, that lay field to field, till there be no place, that they may be placed alone (monopoly) in the midst of the earth."

Scan your own radio dial sometime and check out what you hear in the radio grotto. The locally owned, independent, family oriented radio stations are gone for the most part, having been gobbled up by the corporate giants (the real pirates.).

Back in the 80's I tried to start a radio station. We made application to the FCC, hired an engineer, we went through all the hoops on two different occasions. Like many others before me, I found it to be an exercise in futility. Believe me, when I say, if you don't have millions of dollars and a congressman or two in your back pocket - forget it.

Then a few years ago we discovered that the FCC had stopped licensing stations that run less than 100 watts of power. My attorney and I concluded that if we ran 95 watts of power (the average fm station runs 3000 watts or more) we couldn't be charged with unlicensed operation, since the FCC had stopped Class D 100 watt licensing.

We have since modified our legal arguments, but the bottom line is - on November 3rd 1996 Radio Free Lenawee went on the air providing programming not available anywhere else. I can honestly say that in that time period we never harmed anyone else's right to use the air space. In fact at a recent hearing in Federal District Court in Detroit the local chairman of the FCC admitted under oath, that after five years of our station being on the air, they had no complaints on record alleging our station caused any technical interference. Later, I discovered that the only people who were pushing the FCC to get us off the air were the owners of a local station that features Country Western music.

That's it.

As I write this, an injunctive order forbids us from broadcasting. Our loyal audience, that we estimate to be upwards of 15,000 people are now denied their right to hear their station because a couple of local station owners could "wag the dog" and use the gun barrel of the government to stop us.

We are back in Federal Court awaiting a jury trial on the merits of our case. From the beginning, I knew there would be a battle to keep the station up and running. On the first day of broadcasting Radio Free Lenawee, I promised our listening audience that if we could ever get a fair and honest court to hear our position on the radio issue, that I would abide by that court's ultimate ruling. We are now in that process. All those who love freedom and Radio Free Lenawee desire your prayers for a just outcome.

I have a friend who is British who also claims he is an Israelite and that he is not a Jew. Is he nuts? How can this possibly be?

I don't know if he is nuts or not, but what he is claiming is what is commonly referred to as Israel Identity.

When Israel's King Solomon died, there basically followed a tax rebellion wherein ten tribes which came to be known as the Kingdom of Israel, pulled away and migrated North. This action left the tribes of Benjamin, Judah and part of Levi in the South, who came to be known as the Kingdom of Judah with its capital in Jerusalem.

What became of the migrating Israelites is a matter of some controversy. Many believe that they can historically trace their migration through the Caucasus Mountains, thence into Spain, Germany, and North into Scandinavia and particularly, as in the case of your friend, the British Isles. Later they migrated to North America as the pilgrims.

> Arthur Koestler, makes a clear and convincing case that the majority of people who call themselves Jews today, are not even descended from Israel

Many well-documented and well-researched books have been written on the subject of Israel's migrations. Among the proofs that adherents to this belief offer, is the claim that as Israel migrated North through the Caucasus they lost their identity as Israelites and became known as Caucasians.

Spain was originally called the Iberian Peninsula. Iberia is a variation of the Hebrew name Eber, from which we get the term Hebrew. Israelites are descended from Eber, and therefore they are Hebrews. Evidently, at one time, what we today call Spain, was predominantly populated with Hebrews, or Ibers.

The adjective, "British" is formed from two Hebrew words, "Bryth" which means covenant, and "Ish" which means people. Hence, the British are revealed as "covenant people." Israelites are the only covenant people known in history.

Your friend, while making claim to being Israelite, denies being a Jew because "Israelite" and "Jew" are not synonymous terms, although they are often used interchangeably. After the split in the Kingdom, the Israelites were never referred to as Jews. In fact, the Judahites in the Southern Kingdom were not called Jews in original scripture, but, rather, Yahudin or Judahite. Research shows the term Jew to be rather modern in its derivation and use and not ancient at all.

Further, respected Jewish Author, Arthur Koestler, in his New York Times best-selling book, "The Thirteenth Tribe," (published by Random House) makes a clear and convincing case that the majority of people who today, call themselves Jews, are not even descended from Jacob/Israel. Koestler claims most Jews are of the Asiatic tribe of the Khazars who migrated West to Palestine around 700 AD and simply amalgamated with Judah, adopting her language, history and religion, and in time called themselves "Jews."

If Koestler is right, this might explain why many Jews so naturally reject the gospel and are unmoved by it. Jesus said, "My sheep hear my voice..." They don't hear him because they are not his sheep. Whereas, the Lord also said in Matthew 10:6,

"I am not sent but to the lost sheep of the House of Israel."

The lost or scattered sheep of Israel (like your friend you refer to in your question) have historically responded to the gospel of Jesus Christ, the Gentle Shepherd, in large numbers.

This controversy of Israel and the Jews, that seems to be such a sensitive point with some folks, really gets interesting when you consider Revelation 2:9 where the Lord says,

".. I know the blasphemy of them which <u>say they are Jews, and are not</u> but are the synagogue of Satan."

Who does Jesus refer to in Revelation 2:9 above, that call themselves Jews but are not? Could they be Koestler's Khazars?

The Bible tells us that the Jews are God's chosen people, and Christians have a duty to bless and support them. I get really mad when I hear some preachers say that the Jews are not his chosen. Are these preachers just ignorant, anti-Semitic or what?

Don't get mad. Get informed. Have you ever found a verse in the Bible that stated the Jews are God's chosen people? You can look, but you will not find it. Contrary to popular opinions, it's just not there.

I feel your confusion stems from your assumption that the words Jew and Israelite have the same meaning. They do not. For the sake of argument, let's say the name Jew referred to the descendents of the tribe of Judah. Judah was only one tribe of twelve. Even if that were true, and there is no hard evidence to indicate that that is true; then what would the other eleven tribes be known as? Nowhere in the Bible has the twelve tribe nation of Israel ever collectively been called Jews.

Furthermore, I think you are confused about God's promise to Abraham and the meaning of Genesis 12:2,3

"And I will make of thee a great nation,....and I will bless them that bless thee, and curse him that curseth thee; and in thee shall all families of the earth be blessed."

This is the first covenant God made with Abraham. It indeed makes him a chosen person and it speaks of a coming "great nation," that would be descended from Abraham, but in no way does it refer to Jews.

Let me caution you, not to fall into the trap of assuming something to be fact, simply because you were told it by a respected religious leader, or heard it on TV. Study the scriptures and make sure you are being told the truth.

There were no Jews at the time of the making of this covenant with Abraham. Genesis 12 above, is a promise to Abraham and his yet unborn nation. In fact, Abraham had no children at the time of this promise. Israel was not a nation. There weren't even any Arabs yet, who by the way, are also Abraham's seed through Hagar.

In Deuteronomy 7:6 God said this of Israel "….thou art an holy people unto the Lord thy God; the LORD thy God hath chosen thee to be a special people unto himself, above all people that are upon the face of the earth,"

I will agree, that Israel is chosen of God. But I urge you to not confuse Jews with Israelites. The world is painfully aware that there is a political subdivision in Palestine, that since 1948 has been recognized by the United Nations and the world in general as the State of Israel. However, there is much controversy that exists surrounding the legitimacy of the claim that the current occupiers, who call themselves Jews, make.

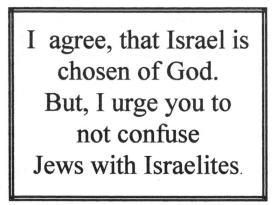

I agree, that Israel is chosen of God. But, I urge you to not confuse Jews with Israelites.

Revelation 2:9 "I know the blasphemy of them which say they are Jews, *and are not*, but are of the synagogue of Satan."

In all of my life's experience, I know of only one people who have made a constant claim to being "God's chosen people." Who can this scripture above, possibly be referring to?

Weren't we told in Genesis 12, that if we bless Abraham's seed we will be blessed?

Since 1948 our U.S. Government has given billions of dollars in aid and "blessing" to the mini-state of Israel, all with the urging of the establishment's televangelists who preach on Jewish dominated, FCC controlled, television and radio airwaves.

If the Jews in Palestine are God's chosen people, then surely, after over 50 years of us blessing them, the United States should be a really blessed land! Lets take a look and see. Since 1948 The United States of America, the formerly undisputed, most powerful nation in World history has seen the following:

- Its financial status as a world power brought down to nearly bankrupt levels.
- We were once the richest nation on earth, we are now the world's largest creditor.
- Jewish lawyers have removed the Ten Commandments and prayer from our schools.
- Real education has declined, kids seem dumber than ever.
- Schools are war-zones with shootings and bombings.
- Vietnam and other phony, no-win wars have killed and maimed over 100,000 of our best youth.
- Drugs like cocaine, heroine, and alcohol plague our land.
- People go nuts and shoot up factories and public places with no rhyme or reason.
- We can't build prisons fast enough, while we currently imprison more of our own people than any other nation on the face of the earth.
- Crime is rampant.
- Liberals in government are bent on taking our firearms, leaving law-abiding citizens further defenseless against criminals who are so brazen, they now invade houses, and commit car-jackings in broad daylight.
- Cancer and other diseases escape a cure, everyone seems to be

sick with something.

- The divorce rate has risen five fold since 1948 to beyond the 50% failure level.
- Pornography floods the media and over 60% of internet sites are pornographic.
- As I write this, America is in a serious financial recession. Downsizing and mergers leave more thousands unemployed on a daily basis.
- Our borders are open to illegal aliens to come in by the thousands daily.
- Environmentalist tree huggers have our natural resources hog tied, and economically strangled.
- New York City, and Washington D.C. have been attacked by fanatics who hijacked the controls of four commercial airplanes. The terrorists tell us their declared hatred of the United States is rooted in our country's lopsided support for Israel!
- Our entire foreign policy is directly in opposition to George Washington's warning to never get involved in the domestic affairs of a foreign government. Here we are George, up to our necks everywhere around the world!
- Academy Awards are given to immoral actroids who mock God, the Christian religion and everything holy, then we stupid Americans pay good money to go to theatres and "be entertained by this trash!"
- Blaring Rock and Roll music enhanced by drugs, bump and grind our youth into sexual oblivion resulting in a generation of babies having babies and spreading sexually transmitted diseases at the same time.

Prior to 1948 America was undeniably blessed. The whole world knew it. We were undefeatable. Economically strong. Morally fit. We lead the world in virtually every industry. But not today.

How much more has to happen before we realize we are not being blessed!

I offer this for your consideration. The next time someone says we must bless and support the Jewish mini-state of Israel, because of the Abrahamic covenant of Genesis 12, stop them. Insist that they show you where we have been blessed by God, since we as a nation have engaged in 50 years of lopsided, highly biased and truly racist behavior in supporting the Jewish mini-state calling itself Israel.

This is addressed elsewhere within this book, but, for now, let me show you, from the New Testament, whom God has chosen.

God's chosen people, are Jesus Christ himself and all the believers in Jesus Christ.

- Luke 23:35 "Christ, the *chosen* of God."
- Mark 13:20 "The elect whom he hath *chosen*."
- John 6:70 " I have *chosen* you twelve."
- John 15:16 "Ye have not chosen me, but I have
- *chosen* you."
- John 15:19 "I have *chosen* you out of the world."
- Acts 22:14 "God of our fathers hath *chosen* (Paul)."
- Galatians 3:16 "Now unto Abraham and his seed were the promises made. He saith not, and to seeds, as of many, but as of one, And to thy seed, which is Christ
- Acts 16:13 "Salute Rufus *chosen* in the Lord
- Eph 1:4 " According as he hath *chosen* us in him "
- II Thessalonians 2:13 "Because God hath from the beginning *chosen* you (believers in Thessalonica) to salvation,...."
- I Peter 2:9 ,10 "but you (believers) are a *chosen* generation, a royal priesthood, an holy nation... which in time past were not a people are now the people of God."
- Rev. 17:14 "they that are with him (the risen, glorified Christ) are called, and *chosen* and faithful.

There you have it. In the end of time, the true, chosen people, are with Christ.

I am Chinese. The Chinese can trace their dynasties back 14,000 years. How can Christian preachers say that man has existed on earth for only about 6000 years?

Its easy. Preachers, are for the most part, well-meaning people who teach what they were taught in Bible school. Sometimes, if it's advantageous, they can be tempted to lean towards the prevailing position that is politically correct also. Don't be too hard on preachers. They are just people. Generally they mean well, even when they are wrong.

You might be surprised to know that I agree with you that the Chinese have probably been here for 14,000 years or more. Adam made his debut on the scene of time more recently, about 6000 years ago.

Traditionalist Christians, will at first, find it difficult to accept that what I am saying, is completely in harmony with scripture. Making an admission that Adam was not the first man on the planet, as true as it may be, is not in harmony with political correctness, or establishment religion.

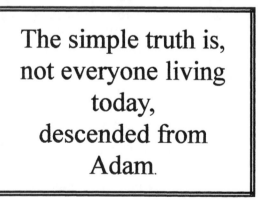

The simple truth is, not everyone living today, descended from Adam.

The 6000 year calculation comes from the Biblically verifiable fact that Adam was formed approximately 4000 years before Christ. Christ was 2000 years ago. You add the two together, and there you have Adam's 6000 year timeline.

I am sure you are aware that at one time everyone "knew" the world was flat. That is, until it was discovered that it was round. Similarly, Copernicus said the Sun, not the earth, was the center of our solar system and was nearly burned at the stake for blasphemy.

Did you know that thousands of sailors died of scurvy until it was discovered that vitamin C found in limes would cure and prevent it? It only took the experts within the medical community 400 years to accept that little fact of life.

What am I saying? Just this. Sometimes it takes a long time, for simple truths to come to widespread acceptance. The Simple truth is, not everyone living today, came from Adam.

The books of Genesis and Ezekiel make it clear that Adam and Eve were not the first people on this planet. The Chinese and other distinct lines of people were already here. But, to see it that way, you must accept the scripture for what it actually says, rather than buying into the politically correct theological mythology which maintains that everyone currently living, came from Adam.

Before I go right to the heart of the "origin and spread of man issue," it is important for me to share a couple of research tips. Jesus Christ, the master teacher, shared some principles of discovery with us. Principles such as "ask and you shall receive, seek and ye shall find, knock and it shall be opened. " Bible truths are not always readily apparent to the casual observer.

Jesus taught in parables and without the "key" you cannot understand them. As with the parables Jesus taught, the rest of the Word of God is often veiled or shrouded with mystery, so that the truth of any given matter, is not always readily apparent. Jesus told his disciples,

"..it is given unto you to know the mysteries of the kingdom of heaven, but to them it is not given....they have closed their eyes, ...but blessed are your eyes because they see......" (Matthew 13:11-16)

This was Jesus' explanation for why he taught in parables. The matters of the Kingdom are only for certain chosen eyes to perceive. God's inspired writers of Genesis and other Old Testament books were no doubt lead by the Father to write in "mystery form," in much the same way as the parables of Jesus were presented in veiled sentences.

"To whom is the arm of the Lord revealed...? (Isaiah 53:1)

Isaiah 28:9 & 10 provides a key insight into how most Bible revelation comes to us.

"...to whom shall he teach knowledge,...and make to understand

> # The book of Genesis in the Old Testament is like the Book of Revelation in the New Testament in that they both contain an amount of symbolism.

doctrine? Precept must be upon precept,.... line upon line... here a little and there a little..."

Isaiah told us above, that the puzzle parts come to us by piecemeal. "Here a little, there a little." A little nugget of insight from Ezekiel, put together with a piece in Genesis, and, voila, a picture begins to form.

The book of Genesis in the Old Testament is like the Book of Revelation in the New Testament in that they both contain an amount of symbolism. A symbolic talking snake, fruits that have intelligence and angels with flaming swords, all appear in the midst of a Garden full of trees.

In the book of Ezekiel, chapter 31, nations of people are depicted as <u>trees</u>. The Assyrian was a Cedar in Lebanon. Additionally, this chapter mentions the other Cedars, Chestnut and the Fir Trees that are all identified as being in the *Garden of God*. The location of the Garden of God is identified unmistakably in verse 9 where we read the *"Trees of Eden* .. (were).. in the Garden of God. Furthermore, Ezekiel makes symbolic mention of the height of the trees in proportion to national greatness and the significance of the rivers and tributaries. Verse four is a picture straight out of Genesis Chapter 2. The trees in the garden are symbolic of nations of people living at the same time Adam was created out of the dust of the earth.

Critics of this type of study will say that, "God says what he means and means what he says. God has no intention for these matters to be 'hidden' and in need of 'deciphering'."

I have no reply to those kind of people. It's nearly impossible to have meaningful discourse with people whose minds and hearts are not open to consider a new view. Have you ever run up against someone who had their arms folded up against their chest proclaiming "My mind is made up! Don't confuse me with the facts?"

Jesus certainly knew what this was like when his critics said,

"We plainly heard him say he would destroy the temple and rebuild it in three days" Is that what Jesus said? That is what they plainly heard. Do you get my point? Jesus also said we must eat his flesh and drink his blood. Is he a cannibal? Of course not, he was speaking forward in time to his last supper. You see, not everything spoken or in print is literal, is it?

When Adam was formed, God said "there is not a man to till the ground." There were men for other purposes, but Adam was the first agriculturalist. Have you ever noticed that many non-Adamic peoples of the world would starve without Adam's descendents to produce over half the world's food resources. Not everybody can farm successfully. But Adam could and his descendants still do.

Later, when Cain slew Able his brother, he said to God, "every man who finds me will slay me." If we accept the prevailing notion about Adam being the first man on the planet, and no Chinese (nor anyone else, for that matter) anywhere yet, then this statement really makes no sense. Who is

> "there is not a man to till the ground."
>
> There were men for other purposes, but Adam was the first agriculturalist.

"every man" that supposedly is going to kill Cain? Were Cain's mother and father going to kill him? Get real.

Cain knew what lay outside the borders of his safe family environment. There was a bunch of people beyond those borders that Cain was not related to, and evidently from Cain's comment, he perceived they were not particularly nice either. Who were they? All those nations depicted by the trees, possibly including the fierce warrior tribes of the Orient (the Chinese).

This is the real clincher. God sent Cain, East to a land called Nod and there he married a *wife*. (Genesis 4:16 & 17.) If everyone descended from Adam and Eve, where did she come from? The answer is, she was already there. Because Adam, Eve and Cain were not the first people on our planet. The Chinese, the dwellers in Nod (and others no doubt) were already occupying the planet.

Politically corrected theologians try to argue that Cain married his cousin many years later and that's who his wife was, but that is speculative, illogical and there is nothing in scripture to remotely suggest that.

It is well established, that the Chinese people have a demonstrated history of mathematical abilities. Consider their invention of the abacus, an early prototype of a calculator. Is accurate time keeping also a part of the science of math? Of course it is. So you see, practically speaking, the Chinese certainly could and probably do, have dynasties that go back many thousands of years before Adam

There is an objection to this revelation that often comes up from preachers, who have no other explanation for why they reject this teaching, other than the potential dilemma it presents for non-Adamites. They will say, "Ok, if this is all true, then the other non-Adam nations would not need salvation would they?" I beg to differ. Romans 5:14 reveals,

"Nevertheless death reigned from Adam to Moses, EVEN OVER THEM THAT HAD NOT KNOWN SIN AFTER THE SIMILITUDE OF ADAM'S TRANSGRESSION."

Adam's fall hit us all. There's only one God. Whoever is here on this planet is part of God's creation and we're all in the same soup. According to God's word we're all equally in need of the Savior!

It is so much more spiritually satisfying to read the Bible and accept the Word of God for what it says, than to buy into clearly illogical, politically corrected lines of thinking to please men. Truth and honesty are much better than myth and fantasy. By the way, I've mentioned political correctness several times. Continue on with the discussion of the Flood and you will see more clearly what I mean.

"The opposite of what is commonly believed is often the truth."

Jean de La Bruyere circa. 1695

***A friend told me that Noah's Flood in Genesis was
local and didn't cover the entire globe.
Where'd he get that crazy idea?***

Probably from the Bible.

Just as the commonly perpetuated story of Adam being the first and only man created and placed on this earth, has a political expediency connected to it, even so, does the common interpretation that the Genesis flood covered the entire planet, have a political motive connected to it.

We shall first of all, take up a scriptural discussion as to why the Bible does not teach a global flood, then we will discuss the reason why the global flood myth is so prevalent.

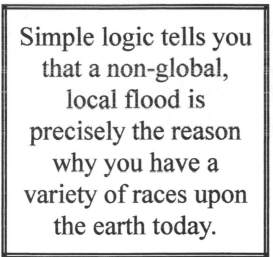

Simple logic tells you that a non-global, local flood is precisely the reason why you have a variety of races upon the earth today.

Please bear in mind that the following view of what happened during the time of the Genesis flood, is in no way a questioning of what God is *able* to do. God creates universes, he speaks worlds into existence. He has all power and authority. If he wants to cover the planet with water until the Sun is floating - he is able. The scripture is clear that the flood, while vast in its coverage, was still a relatively local event and not global, and that some people like the Chinese and others were to varying degrees, not affected by it.

Simple logic tells you that a non-global, local flood is precisely the reason why you have a variety of races upon the earth today. If the flood covered the entire planet and only Noah's family survived, everyone living today would be of the same genetic racial tree. But, we're not. There is a vast genetic difference between the races and particularly between Asians, Caucasians, and Africans.

No genetic scientist worth his salt, would suggest that the major races of people that inhabit this planet sprang from one man's loins, and they didn't. To teach otherwise is not scientific. It doesn't make sense. Most importantly, it's not what the Bible teaches.

The Genesis flood of waters was upon the "erets."

The key to the revelation that the flood was local and not global is the Hebrew word translated earth. If you go to your Strong's Concordance and look up the word earth you will find it is number 776 in Strong's Hebrew dictionary. The Hebrew word that was translated "earth" is erets.

Erets means = earth, field, land, ground or country.

It is the same word used in Genesis when Moses returned to the erets (land) of Egypt. Abraham was told by God to "Get thee out of thy erets (country) and from thy father's house, unto a erets (land) that I will show thee. Jacob dwelt in the erets (land) wherein his father was a stranger, the erets (land) of Canaan. Notice that in each case "erets" describes a locality, not the entire planet.

Cain, when he was judged by God after killing Able said, "You have driven me this day from the face of the erets (earth)" (Genesis 4:14)

Did you think God sent him off the planet to Mars or to the Moon? He was driven off the face of the earth wasn't he? But the word is <u>erets</u>, it means land, or that locality.

Incidentally, Cain then "went out from the presence of the Lord, and dwelt in the <u>erets</u> (land) of Nod." If you check, you will find that "erets" appears over 2400 times in scripture and in virtually every single verse it refers to a specific area of land or country, including Genesis chapters 6 and 7 where the " flood of waters was upon the <u>erets</u> (earth)." The flood was massive, but it did not cover the planet.

There have been many geologic upheavals which have left evidences of flooding around the globe. Whale bones have been found in deserts in North America and other places. Proponents of the global flood cite these examples to support their position. Personally, I think an honest reading of Word of God, together with God-given logic, make better sense.

You'll also notice that, up until the flood you have a complete Adamic genealogy of the relatives of Adam and his descent to Noah. After the flood, just nine generational links later, Abram comes on the scene. He encounters a bunch of new people, heretofore unmentioned in scripture, such as, Amraphel King of Shinar, Arioch King of Ellasar, Chedorlaomer King of Elam and Tidal King of Nations. Additionally, we are introduced to people called Sodomites, Rephaims, the Zuzims and Imims, the Horites and on and on. People, who I assure you were aliens to Abram, not killed by the flood and not likely Adamite.

The flood came because the racial integrity of the Adam seed-line was in danger of disruption by the non-Adamites "taking wives of all that they chose." Noah was perfect in his genealogy, but, God had to "hose" down the area (erets) where he lived in order to assure the fact that the promised seed could travel down the generational line, genealogically intact, all the way to the virgin

Mary. She, of course, would eventually bear the promised redemptive seed of Jesus Christ.

Satan's religious zeal for a utopian ideal - equality.

The children of darkness are religiously passionate about an unattainable ideal called "equality." This stems from their unwritten, almost subconsciously accepted belief, in a universal brotherhood of man embraced by a universal fatherhood of god. These twin fundamental principals are essential ingredients that make up their world view. Why? Because, if everyone did not spring from Adam, if other races pre-existed or co-existed, then there might be some naturally occurring differences or inequalities between the races. Notice, I did not say superiority or inferiority - just differences. Ardent devotees of political correctness and universal equality, nearly go mad at the mere mention of such possibilities.

Bible believers are already aware of the fact, that God defined specific class, status, personality and character predispositions that would genetically follow certain ethnic lines. For instance,

"Ishmael (father of the Arabs) . shall be a *wild* man; his hand shall be against every man, and every man's hand against him..." (Genesis 16:11,12)

Speaking of Jacob and Esau,

"...two manner of people shall be separated from thy womb, the one people shall be stronger than the other people; and the elder (Esau) shall serve the younger (Jacob)." (Genesis 25:23)

New Age, liberal idealist types, reject any such notions as racial or ethnic stereo-typifying. As a consequence of rejecting such Biblically recorded facts of life, they also, by default, reject God and his Word.   The book you are reading, <u>Without Controversy</u> is a book about truth, not about re-writing reality.

Ever since Satan was cast out of heaven (thus he became unequal) and the revolution in the Garden took place, Satan, the Serpent has been obsessed with equality.   When you are obsessed to obtain what you can never have, you go crazy.   Satan is crazy! Satan can never be equal with God.   Yet, he obsesses to attain this unattainable utopia and induces all who follow his rebellions, to adopt his convoluted and illogical beliefs, all of which are religious.

Even when his teachings are found in educational text books under the guise of science or philosophy, they are religious in nature.   Evolution is the obvious example.   Under the guise of science, the myth of evolution is a direct challenge to God's sovereign claim to creation.   Isn't it clever, how Satan's doctrines are taught, embraced and go unchallenged as fact, in academic circles?   We don't recognize educators as religious figures, but, in reality, they are.

In fact, everyone is religious.   A person's religion is simply the set of ideas they embrace about the realities of life.   Whatever values guide your beliefs about what is good or bad, what is normal or not normal, what is right or wrong, constitutes your religion. Everything in life is religious, because virtually everything in one way or another deals with the ultimate realities of this life.   That is why it is impossible for public education to be religiously neutral. More on this later.   For now, let's get back to the equality scam.

Widespread sensitivity training has been implemented to ensure that less and less, will ever be said openly, about differences in any two or more groups. Just dare to openly suggest that there's a significant difference between men and women in any area of life and the National Organization of Women will be out in full protest.

But men and women are different. We're all different. Everyone knows it by nature. We just don't dare to say it. Why is that?

Have we all gotten so open-minded our brains have fallen out? No two men are equal. No two women are equal. No two snow flakes are equal. No two athletes are equal. If they were, there would be no point in having a contest. If we know this in the natural and practical world, then why do we give so much credence and silent acquiescence to the false notion of equality in any other facet of life?

Is it because of the methodical, brain numbing effect of television and other media personalities, endlessly harping on equality issues on a continuous basis? Admit it, when authoritative and respected media icons serve up sensitive issues in hallowed and sacred terms, you're seen as a "secular sinner" if you don't bow down before the "altar of equality" and genuflect. Just, what, does happen, if you don't bow down?

If you don't accept homosexuality as being on an equal par with heterosexuality or if you find women trying to get into military combat roles to be inappropriate or if you believe any of the equality crowd's sacred cows are illogical or Biblically unacceptable and dare to say so, look out! Get ready to be demonized as a "closed-minded, racist, hateful, homophobe, insensitive, intolerant" or a host of other names. Names which are carefully crafted to impart political pain and stigmatize the hapless recipients, leaving him or her socially damaged and smarting from the effects. Imagine how you would feel, if a newspaper headline featuring your name, accused you, of being a racist.

That is about all the politically correct crowd has in its arsenal. Names and name calling. No one can defend Satanically inspired, mythological equality with any sense of logic. Equality does not exist in the real world. It never did, and it never will. The problem is, most pointy-headed idealists that promote universal equality, don't live in the real world.

The doctrine of universal equality in all things is a Satanically inspired weapon used to disrupt and destroy a world of sound reason, in order that Satan and his minions can pursue the utopian goal of creating a universal New World Order. The master-mind of the Anti-Christ insists

> We must all be equally brain-washed. Equally dumbed down. Equally quiet, subservient and submissive.

that there be no dissent in the ranks. We must all be equally brain-washed. Equally dumbed down. Equally quiet, subservient and submissive.

Every man, woman, boy, and girl must be thoroughly indoctrinated (educated) with the principle that we are all equal. Taken to the extreme, the equality crowd believes that whales, trees, dogs and cats are all on an equal par with humans. If you have ever had a run in with a "save the whales" or environmentalist tree-hugger type you know what I mean.

These, "we who know what's best for you," humanist types, are actually quite religious, some are even fervent. Their religion is exercised by pursing the utopian goal of universal world government, world peace, with one world economy, and, of course, unattainable worldwide equality.

Professor Allan Bloom, in his best-selling book, The Closing of the American Mind, (Simon & Schuster) said this of today's students. "They are unified only in their relativism and in their allegiance to equality. And the two are related in a moral intention. The relativity of truth is not a theoretical insight but a moral postulate, the condition of a free society, or so they see it. They have all been equipped with this framework early on, and it is the modern replacement for the inalienable natural rights that used to be the traditional American grounds for a free society......The danger they have been taught to fear from absolutism, is not error, but intolerance. ....The purpose of their education is not to make them scholars but to provide them with a moral virtue- openness.

Notice how Professor Bloom so clearly summarizes in almost religious tones, the state of mind of a significant number of present day college students. They haven't been educated, they have been indoctrinated or "equipped." He also rightly describes their "allegiance to equality." The indoctrination process called public education, instead of graduating scholars, rather, produces a new religious specie. One that is tolerant of everything, accepts no absolutes, questions everything traditional, rejects everything that is ancient or rooted in history as not being evolutionarily relevant. They are convinced that in "closing their mind," they are actually open-minded and they bear unswerving allegiance to a myth called, "equality."

Modern education is amazingly successful in creating secular humanist atheists, or at least, agnostics, who readily buy into the concept and wholeheartedly support the perpetuation of, a politically correct, new world order. But not everyone currently living, functioning and voting in our society is fully indoctrinated. Some are religious.

In order to assure ultimate success, the architects and implementers of the Satanic world order, must capture and subdue, not only, secular society through mass education, but at least for the short term, they need the support of Christians and their ministers. Those ministers must, reliably and unquestioningly, teach their flocks that everybody living on planet earth, originally came from Adam. This elementary belief, together with the teaching that the Genesis flood killed everybody on the whole planet, except for the ark occupants, is fundamental to Satan's long-term plan. These two teachings help minimize any likelihood that the Christian community will be of any serious hindrance to the devil's global world order.

With these two basic beliefs unchallenged and deeply entrenched in the believer's mind, one conclusion is established and inescapable. No matter how far removed from Adam we may be, or what race we are, we are all related, and thus, in the most fundamental way, we are all "equal."

As with your immediate family ties and moral obligations, so is it with your global duties. You've heard the old adage, "charity begins at home," haven't you? You share and share alike with your brothers, sisters and cousins don't you? If you are a member of the global family, then, how could you fail to recognize your global responsibilities to meet the needs of your fellow man? You should dig in and share what your nation possesses with the entire brotherhood of man around the world. That is why, as of this writing, America's wealth is being distributed all around the world. Your taxes rise. The nation's debt is out of sight. Your standard of living is constantly shrinking, and our military is scattered to every continent to either deliver global meals on wheels or enforce equality at the muzzle of a gun.

The communist's used to call it the "redistribution of wealth." Winston Churchhill called it the "equal sharing of misery." Hard working and fed-up Americans everywhere call it theft.

The globalist idealists call it "equality" in it's many forms and insist that we all march in lock-step to equality's utopian demands. If you don't keep up, you're out of step.

As Satan merges all the inhabitants of the world into one big global unit, with no national boundaries, no ethnic distinctions, one universal legal system, one universal economy, one world language, one world religion (that will not be Christian.) The result will be one miserable world. That is, unless a Christian freedom movement arises and takes hold on this crazy world.

If Christians ever liberate themselves from the equality scam - Satan will be in real trouble. A sense of nationalism just might return to America, then it would be ok to love your American homeland over and above any other. The embracing of Christianity, as the only valid religion would replace the truly, stupid notion that all religions have value and that we must respect all other religions despite the fact that, Christianity by its very nature is an "exclusive and absolute" religion. Jesus said,

"No man cometh to the Father, but by me." (John 14:6)

Lies would no longer be on an equal par with truth. Moral relativism would be out, along with its illegitimate twin sister situational ethics. Absolutes would return to their rightful place. Wrong would never be right. Homosexuality would cease to be an alternate (thus equal) lifestyle. A normal family would once again be legally recognized as a husband and wife, mother and father with children, not just any two lesbians, or "gay partners." The list could go on and on.

If you are still suffering from the effects of long term "intellectual socialization" induced by the indoctrination process referred to as public education, you no doubt bristle at the notion that anyone would suggest a view of non-equality, or moral absolutism. The effect of long term gradualism is not easily reversed. If you are having a hard time with re-education, don't feel bad. Reclaiming your mind and thinking process takes time.

"..and be not conformed to this world, but be transformed by the renewing of your mind." (Romans 12:2)

112

What does the Bible tell us about equality? You might be surprised.

The Bible is anything but a manual on equality. God declared long ago that his people were to be a superior nation above all nations. That doesn't sound like equality does it? God said " Jacob have I loved, Esau have I hated." (Romans 9:13) Sodom and Gomorrah were not on the good list, they were equal to nothing except abomination. What about the Canaanites that God told his people to kill and exterminate. Is God bigoted? Noah was selectively separated from everyone else who was scheduled to die in the flood. Was Noah someone special? You bet he was. Oh my, look how God discriminates!

Was God, a bigot, when he ordered Israel to not make leagues with the other nations and cultures and warning them to not make marriages with them? (Deuteronomy 7:3)

"...Do not intermarry with them. Do not give your daughters to their sons or take their daughters for your sons,....(Deuteronomy 7:3 NIV)

Sounds strange to think of God as a racist doesn't it? Read your Bible. What did he tell Israel?

God didn't want his people marrying anyone but Israelites. (Ezra 9:2,12) Isn't that what we've all been taught constitutes racism? The news media and the fanatics of equality constantly echo, "Everyone is equal. Marry anyone you want. God's law means nothing. You can disregard every cultural line. Throw out every limit. Limits are only there to create impediments to freedom and further equality."

If you want to have some fun and don't fear what people think of you, try this. I dare you to stand up in your church and announce that you have recently discovered that according to modern university standards, God is a racist. You will never be viewed as sane again.

According to Satan, God is not only a racist, he also discriminates. Look at this.

"…The Lord your God has chosen you out of all the peoples on the face of the earth (erets) to be his people, his treasured possession." (Deuteronomy 7:6)

"…a people that are <u>above all the nations</u> that are upon the earth." (Deuteronomy 14:2)

No wonder the spirit of this world hates God and his disdain of equality. Sinners are not equal to saints. The saved are not equal with the lost. Murderers and thieves are not equal to the law abiding. Sodomites are not equal with heterosexuals. No book is equal to the Bible. Jesus Christ stands alone in his superiority and true Israel is a superior nation of people, all because God says so.

Satan, that old serpent in the Garden, was the first proponent of equality. He said, "ye shall be <u>as</u> gods." (Genesis 3:5) "As, means equal to." In effect, the Devil's argument was, "you don't need God, you can be *equal* to a god." Ever since God judged the Serpent and thus made him *not equal* he has detested inequality! He lusts for equality!

In order to fall into the confusion of all the political correctness that has permeated our society today, you must put aside and ignore these obvious truths I am talking about in this little book. Please don't put truth aside, embrace it.

Now, frankly, in this new millennium we are in, It doesn't matter what race you are, or how superior or inferior you may feel you are. I just want the record to be clear that the Bible is true. The Devil is a liar, and he has spread his lies everywhere. It's imperative that people learn the truth and be delivered from politically correct myths.

It does make a difference what people believe about equality. You may not yet believe it really is any big deal, but trust me on this one, Satan sure thinks it's a big deal. His system and its adherents are tirelessly promoting it all the time.

Christians used to be able to muster something called "righteous indignation." They would get righteously mad and stand up and defend their beliefs in the face of insult. Increasingly, though, Christians are succumbing to an anemic passivity, while the children of darkness are the ones that speak-up, protest, and demand that you bow down, value, embrace and give respect to the tenets of their belief system. You may be insulted by some of what I am saying here, but deep inside you know it's the truth.

The more you stretch your mind and filter all your thinking through a spiritual sieve, the more you realize how religious the whole world is. The struggles of this world are the result of clashing religious views, the competition of gods. Satan and his world view, versus The Lord God and his world view, is the big game in town.

Where are you in all this? Are you in the game, or on the sideline?

"Whosoever therefore shall be ashamed of me and of my words in this adulterous and sinful generation: of him also shall the Son of man be ashamed when he cometh..." (Mark 8:38)

I read a newspaper article that said my favorite Christian minister is anti-Semitic and preaches hate, and that the Bible itself is a book of hate and not love. How can they get away with saying such things?

If there were newspapers in Jesus' day the headlines would have read,

"Jesus Mother Linked to Scandal with Roman Solder"

" False Messiah Uses Tricks and Magic to Swindle the Ignorant"

"Jesus - Associated with Harlots and Criminals."

"Felony Warrants Sought After Riot Incited at Temple Treasury."

"Conspiracy to Bomb Temple Uncovered - Jesus Implicated."

"We wrestle not against flesh and blood but against powers and principalities, the rulers of the darkness of this present world." (Ephesians 6:12)

Jesus said, "If they have called me, the master of the House Beelzebub, how much more they of his household." and "Beware when all men speak well of you, for so did your fathers of the false prophets." (Matt 10:25, Luke 6:26)

Today everyone from Rush Limbaugh to Jerry Falwell has been

accused at one time or another of being racist, bigoted, homophobic or anti-Semitic. So, I don't feel too lonely in being the target of the mudslingers.

> " The word anti-Semitic doesn't even have a definition. No one seems to know exactly what it means, except - trouble."
>
> **Syndicated writer- Joe Sobran**

The anti-Semitic name is an interesting one. I like what syndicated columnist Joe Sobran said, " The word anti-Semitic doesn't even have a definition. No one seems to know exactly what it means, except - trouble."

The propagandist of Jesus day were constantly at work trying to sew discord and rumor about the Lord wherever they could. Nothing has changed today. People today mindlessly accept as gospel whatever the "talking heads" on television and print media tell them. The sheeple unquestioningly love whom the media elite love, and hate with a loyalty whomever the media finger as unworthy of respect.

My mother used to say, "sticks and stones may break your bones but names will never hurt you." That sounds good mom, but it's still a bummer to see your name besmirched in headlines and on electronic media. They reach the masses by the millions while you're stuck trying to explaining your position one person at a time. The game of catch up can be exasperating. The pressure can sure be horrendous on the wife and kids too.

My First Personal Experience With
Orwell's Big Brother

I remember back in 1984 when my children were very young. I had built an addition to the Church parsonage without obtaining a building permit.

There were a couple of reasons why I did not apply for a building permit. Both were matters of Law. A permit is an official grant of permission, from a higher power to a lesser power, to be able to do something that would otherwise be illegal or unlawful. The house was not in my name. The property was the Lord's, held in trust for him by the Church and I just couldn't bring myself to cast Jesus Christ in the position of a lesser power, asking Caesar's permission to nail some boards together.

In fact, it wasn't that long ago that most communities did not require churches to pay taxes or obtain permits for anything for just that reason. It had to do with a legal principal involving jurisdiction. Everybody seemed to realize that if God was the head of the Church, who could possibly be higher than him and thus hand down a writ of permission?

The Church was historically recognized as a foreign government. The Church property was like an embassy. That's why when the Marines were in pursuit of drug kingpin Manuel Noriega and he ran into the church for "sanctuary" the Marines stopped at the door. Even the Marines respected the fact that they had no lawful authority to invade the sovereign territory of the Catholic Church. In other words they had no jurisdiction.

Secondly, the blind habit of getting licenses for this and licenses for that, so smacks of the old communist regimes of Romania, and The Soviet Union that I just couldn't bring myself to be a practicing communist. So we built without a permit. Yep, you guessed it. It hit the fan.

At ten o'clock at night, just like the old Nazi Gestapo, two Adrian City police officers arrested me at my home and in my bare feet, took me off to jail in handcuffs. The rest is a long story that includes a jury trial, thirteen days in jail, and numerous front page, headline stories about this horrible and ignorant person Rick Strawcutter, who calls himself a preacher but won't get a building permit. What kind of fool can this guy be?

One police officer at the jail said, "Yeah, Pastor Strawcutter upholds everything but the law." I wanted so bad to talk to him about what the "real law" was, but sadly, so many of our modern day television trained "robo-cops" for the most part, really don't care what the true law is.

I knew that if the founding fathers of our country like Washington, Hamilton or Adams, would have been here, there wouldn't have been any problem. But they were all dead. Could they have sacrificed so much, yet in vain. Did they and thousands more give their lives to establish a free republic only to pass it on to a generation that didn't even care to read or understand the history of it?

Orwell in his classic novel "1984" said, "freedom is slavery, war is peace." Is that what we have come to? Is the norm in this life all reversed and backwards and in opposition to everything that is sane and reasonable, and no one seems to know it or care?

While the pressure was bearable for me, it was terrible for the ones I loved. My little eight year old daughter was taunted at school (a Christian school) by classmates saying things like, "Your dad is a bad man," or "The preacher at my church never goes to jail." or "Your father is a criminal."

I was in jail. The newspapers rolled on daily with their

outrageous claims. My little eight year old daughter, cried a lot. My son was a little older, but it was bad for him too. This is America?

My wife was finishing up her teaching degree at the time, and every school shut the door to her for student teaching. They used to call it black-balling. Practically speaking, her association with me, simply left her without the "mark of the beast." In so many ways in this life, if you do not have the "social mark" of compliance and conformity upon your life, you just can't function or easily make progress..

> # Most people are controlled by fear. How about you? Are you controlled by fear?

The system is smart. Revelation 13:4 says of the powers of Anti-Christ,

"who is like the Beast, who is able to make war with him?"

They figured the best way to get to me, was to make life miserable for my family. How do you fight back against a beast like that?

I remember seeing the movie "Roots." Maybe you do too. Do you recall the movie scene where Kunta Kinte refused to answer to his new slave name of Toby? The master tied him to a post right in the middle of town and in front of the whole community including other frightened slaves, he whipped Kunta Kinte mercilessly until he finally uttered the slave name of Toby. That was his first whipping. It wouldn't be his last. My heart still hurts when I recall the movie segment where poor Toby was begging on his knees,

"Please Massa, don't whip me, I'll be a good slave... just please, please Massa don't whip me anymo..."

How about you, dear reader? Are you a good little slave? You don't want a whipping do you?

Times have not changed much. Except, today's slave masters no longer use whips to modify behavior. Today's "plantation" has newspapers and television to whip all of us contemporary slaves into compliance. The job they do of keeping us in line is truly amazing. Just the thought of anything in print or television being brought to bear against your good name - should you fail to "tow the line," is generally enough to guarantee universal compliance in our modern slave population. Keep in mind, it is not necessary that the media do anything personal, to you, to be affective. Just the potential of something bad or embarrassing being said about you is usually enough to keep the average person in compliance with status quo. The cumulative effect of years of gradual conditioning, is enough to curb any potential dissident behavior among the masses. The status quo is, "Just do as you are told, keep your mouth shut and all will go well."

> Of course, its hard for anybody to get the "big picture," when the local media is in full control of what is viewed

Most people are controlled by fear. How about you? Are you controlled by fear?

Funny thing in all this. Back when the city jailed me on the building code violation, I was naïve enough think that people, by and large, would readily see the "big picture" in what was really happening. I mean really, a pastor jailed in America for an act of conscience? Of course, its hard for anybody to get the "big picture," when the local media is in full control of what is viewed

How the addition was built, from a construction standpoint, was never much of an issue. It was a great building. Built beyond the BOCCA code of standards. People could drive by an see it. What passersby saw was a nice addition, built by accomplished builders. The issue was control It was all about the little piece of paper, the permit. The little paper that constituted a statement that basically says "I bow down and worship you, and I respect your power, the gun-barrel of government."

Remember how armed, Nazi SS and Stalin's Check Point Charley henchmen, would stop each and every traveler and ask,

"Your papers please….. are your papers in order?"

If your papers were not in order…… you were in big trouble. Forget whether your life is in order. The question then was, and today still is, are your papers in order.

Indeed, flashing lights, pull over….. are your papers in order?

Is this the kind of country you want to live in? Evidently for the masses, it is.

That little episode with the building permit in the late 80's got me marked as a disgruntled slave, that the local plantation masters needed to keep track of and whip every now and then.

My Second Whipping

A few years later I preached a radio sermon on the state of world affairs and Biblically how international banking figured into the spread of world wars and the goal of world government etc. Problem is, I made an analogy between the conflicts Jesus had with the Pharisees of his day and the conflict we have with our modern day Scribes (journalists) and Pharisees (lawyers, judges etc.) The stuff really hit the fan when I quoted Jesus saying to the Jews "....you are of your father the devil...."

Well, a local Jewish doctor took offense. I can't prove it, but I think he got special guidance from the Anti-Defamation League and their propaganda experts. Anyway, he wrote a letter to the editor of our local paper that set off a firestorm of the most vicious hate, vented at me, by way of published letters to the editor. It truly was incredible. Full pages of letters from people of every walk of life denouncing me as a new Hitler, a hatemonger, KKK type and more.

The interesting thing about all the attack on me, was that not one of the writers ever spoke with me before they wrote their letters denouncing me. And, none of them had heard the radio sermon either. They based all their comments on what the Jewish doctor had initially said in his letter. They simply, in robotic fashion, regurgitated what the doctor had said, using all the standard politically correct catch phrases, kissed up to the establishment in dutiful fashion and signed their names to their letters.

A local ministerial association even got into the act and wrote a diatribe denouncing me as a minister, while at the same time elevating and distancing themselves from the likes of me. Consistent with the pattern, they did not call me before writing their letter either. It was so bizarre. During all this, I got a renewed appreciation for the term, "sheeple."

Then one night, what I thought was a nice guy from the community, called me on the phone and in a friendly and engaging way we relaxed and talked for almost an hour about world politics, World War II, the post war treaties, the causes of war and so on. I thought, here's a guy who gets it. Then in a sly way, he asked me a trick question. "Can you think of anything good that Hitler did?" I thought a moment then I replied, "Well, he invented the Volkswagen." We both chuckled.

Two days later he wrote an editorial wherein he said,

"I found Reverend Strawcutter to be a vicious anti-Semite who praises Hitler and hates Jews......"

Somebody said, "You're not paranoid, if they're really out to get you."

Here I was, one preacher. There they were, a newspaper with a hate agenda and an unlimited supply of ink, together with local radio. They spoke to thousands. I spoke to basically one person at a time. What would you have done?

Then I got an idea. I made a 45 minute video tape that responded to what was going on and had my loyal supporters join me in going to the street with signs that said

-----

"Pastor Strawcutter's
Forbidden
Videos - Free."

We passed out 2000 of them all over town. The tape was titled "Media Terrorism and Mind Control." The tape has since become a classic in the national freedom movement. We've sold them all over the United States and even abroad. The video really gave the proponents of truth and Christian liberty a big boost. But at the time it was also expensive and in the long run it was not a really effective way to counteract a local newspaper. But it did have significant impact. People read and then throw out the newspaper, but a good video tape gets viewed, re-viewed and then sometimes gets passed on. So, in that way, we got a lot of mileage from the video.

Somebody said, "Never go to war with someone who buys ink by the barrel." That's Good advice, but we were already at war. What would you have done?

Years later, the Lord showed me how to have my own 24 hour a day radio station. In 1996 Radio Free Lenawee at 99.3 fm was born and finally I had a tool that was more effective than a

> # Life is amazing. One day your just a turd, the next day your on top of the pile

newspaper. We estimated that 20,000 people tuned in the first day. In time, we became the dominant intellectual media. Lenawee County was being liberated.

Respected criminal defense attorney Jim Daly even said,

"No politician in his right mind would think of running for office without being on this radio station, and getting the blessing of this Church."

Our radio station sponsored the only major "Meet the Candidates" forums around election time. We scooped all kinds of news stories. We were on top.

In retreat, the newspaper venom subsided significantly. Actually, the reporters even became friendly. Their reporting became fair and balanced. In political terms, some would say that there had been a shift in the balance of power.

Life is amazing. One day your just a turd, the next day your on top of the pile!

What do you think of the so-called lost books of the Bible?

Oh boy! You just had to ask that one didn't you? Don't you realize that millions of Christians don't even know that such books exist?

The Book of the Wars of the Lord, the Book of Jasher, the Book of the Acts of Solomon, The book of Nathan the Prophet, the Book of Gad the seer, the Book of Shemaikah the Prophet, The Book of Iddo the Seer, The Book of Jehu, the Book of the Records, and the Book of the Purchase are all books mentioned, but not included within the canonized books that make up the modern Christian Bible.

Additionally, Jude vs. 14 states " and Enoch also, the seventh from Adam, prophesied of these, saying, Behold, the Lord cometh with ten thousands of his saints." Enoch prophesied? How did Jude know what Enoch said, unless he had access to a writing by Enoch. If Jude had access to that writing, then why don't we?

We have in our possession a Bible composed of sixty six books bound in one volume. The books that make up the Bible were selected by a committee of Roman priests in the fifth century.

Decisions were made at that time to determine which books were inspired and which ones were not. Those not included were referred to as being spurious. I certainly wouldn't have much confidence in mere men making those kinds of decisions today, and I really have a hard time with spiritual/religious gangsters making those kinds of decisions back then, but, nonetheless, those decisions were made.

I understand, that considerable debate was had on the Book of Daniel and The Book of the Revelation and that both of these books were almost relegated to the spurious category. Had this occurred, you would not have them in your Bible today.

In addition to the books I listed above that are mentioned within the King James Bible, there are a good number of others that exist that are in print today that were not included in the canonization.

I personally enjoy reading the Book of Adam and Eve. Here is one of my favorite passages.

"Again said God unto Adam, "All this misery that thou hast been made to take upon thee because of thy transgression, will not free thee from the hand of Satan, and will not save thee.

> Some people are real passionate about not reading any extra-biblical books.
> "You might get into false doctrine," is the claim.
> I warn you, they are somewhat justified in making that argument!

But I will. When I shall come down from heaven, and shall become flesh of thy seed, and take upon Me, the infirmity from which thou sufferest, then the darkness that came upon thee in this cave shall come upon Me in the grave, when I am in the flesh of thy seed. And I, who am without years, shall be subject to the reckoning of years, of times, of months, and of days, and I shall be reckoned as one of the sons of men, in order to save thee." And God ceased to commune with Adam. (Adam and Eve 14: 3-6)

This writing makes the revelation of the invisible God coming to earth in visible flesh so clear, doesn't it? Do you recall the story in John 21:8 where Peter and his crew had fished all night and had caught nothing? Jesus told them to cast down their net and the net enclosed a large number of fish. The scripture is very specific that the number of fish was 153. I am told that this is the same total number of books that were considered at the time of the canonization. Coincidence? Maybe. I just mention it for your consideration.

Some people are real passionate about not reading any extra-biblical books. "You might get into false doctrine," is the claim. I warn you, that they are somewhat justified in making that argument!

Among the so-called "lost books" are some really bizarre writings that could confuse and perhaps frustrate the faith of some readers. So, from that standpoint, I have some reservations about recommending that everyone read these books.

At the same time, I have faith that the Spirit of Christ guides those who have "ears to hear what the Spirit says." Although I have little time to read these books, I personally don't fear reading them.

You will find a good number of people who not only denounce the "lost books" but they have a very orthodox opinion that the only books you should read are the canonized 66 books. Many of these same people, hold an equally strong opinion about reading only the authorized King James version.

When an individual, group, or denomination adopts a particular view that they feel is sacrosanct, they will invariably bend over backward to build voluminous arguments to support whatever position they feel is right. I guess it's human nature. The matter of reading the King James version, or the canonized 66 Books exclusively is no exception.

Frankly, I find that the truth of God comes through no matter what. Whether I read the Living Bible, the New International Version, the Readers Digest Bible, the Book of Jasher, the Books of Enoch, you name it - I get a blessing out of it.

You shall <u>know</u> the truth and the truth shall make you free. If you have the discerning power of God's Spirit in you, you just *know* when you're reading God's word and when you are not. In all the reading of the lost books that I have done, I have never been persuaded to believe anything that took away from the deity and holiness of our God and the clear plan of salvation laid out in the sixty six books of the Holy Bible.

If you desire to read any of these books (after you have read, and understand the Bible) I would suggest you start with the ones that are mentioned in scripture already, like the Book of Jasher. You'll find it pretty much follows along with the Bible reading you've already done.

Above all, don't fall for the delusional idea that reading the lost books, will some how lead you to discover some fanciful new doctrinal revelation. There's no new revelations. That's not the point of reading them. The 66 books that comprise the Bible we currently have, is more than an ample resource to save the world. I included this question because you're evidently a reader. You have an inquisitive mind. Inquiring minds want to know. Enjoy the journey.

Keep in mind, the Apostles turned the world upside down without printing presses or even a written New Testament. Strive to get the same stuff in your heart that they had, and you'll have everything you'll ever need to do the will of God in your lifetime.

Was the September 11th attack on the World Trade Center predicted in the Bible?

I am not certain that this particular attack was predicted in scripture but, these are some thoughts that might shed some light.

"...shall there be a calamity, in a city and the Lord hath not done it?" (Amos 3:6)

Now, before you get all bent out of shape, thinking "why would God allow something like that to happen?" Let me remind you of how God destroyed the cities of Sodom and Gomorrah for its sin. Many times in Israel's history the enemies of God <u>were allowed by God</u> to invade, destroy and enslave that nation because of their sin and disobedience.

Personally, America's sins and rejection of Christ and his law are so blatant I wouldn't blame God if he totally destroyed this land. Someone once said, "If God doesn't judge America pretty soon, he'll have to apologize to Sodom and Gomorrah." So let's accept the fact that there is no righteous reason why God should place his grace and protection upon us.

Country singing star Charlie Daniels said on national television that he believed "the Lord has pulled back the protective covering to which we have become accustomed." Thus the our enemies were able to get through to our vulnerable areas and hurt us.

I find it interesting that Charlie Daniels, who is not a minister, was not ashamed to voice his opinion, while the Reverend Jerry Falwell initially made a similar statement and then backed up and made an apology. Falwell retracted his earlier claim that the World Trade Center attack was related to God's contempt for this country's pornography, homosexuality and abortion policies. (I wonder who put the pressure on him?)

The Book of Revelation is a good place to look for death and destruction being measured out by God upon the people of the world. Note the apparent reason.

"And the rest...that were not killed by these plagues yet REPENTED NOT of their works of their hands, that they should not worship devils and idols of gold... neither repented they of their sorceries, ... fornication... thefts..." (Revelation 9:20)

Evidently, the whole reason for the plagues (in Revelation) was to bring people to their senses, that they might turn from their sins and repent and start doing what was right. I think we all noticed immediately upon the attack of September 11th how prayer and the mention of God became almost in vogue.

Everybody prayed. The mayor, the president, television newscasters wept openly, sitcoms stopped their idiocy, Letterman and Leno stopped joking, everybody got somber. CBS's Dan Rather broke down and wept openly on Dave Letterman's show. Teachers and students alike, prayed in our schools and other public places, at least for a while. (Christians should take note: If you are praying for revival in America, don't be shocked, but rather, be prepared for more of these kinds of events that tend to bring us to our knees.) This event sure had a spiritual impact!

"Thus saith the Lord, behold, I will raise up against Babylon and against them that dwell in the midst of them that rise up against me, a destroying wind." (Jeremiah 51:1)

The definition of Kamikaze is "a divine destroying wind."

Were the Kamikaze pilots who flew those jets into the Twin Towers, a "divine destroying wind?"

"... that mighty city for in ONE HOUR is thy judgment come." (Revelation 18:10) from the initial attack to the collapse of both buildings was less than one hour.

"Babylon is fallen, is fallen, that great city, because she made all nations drink of the wine of the wrath of her fornication." Revelation 14:8

Does the reference to two fallings imply two buildings?

This great city is described elsewhere in Revelation 18 as the premier world financial hub and the towers, were known as the World Trade Center. Verse 18,

"What city is like this great city?"

How many great cities can there be that are "great" world financial centers?

Revelation refers to this city as Babylon. It just happens that there is a Babylon, New York.

Babylon hath been a golden cup in the LORD'S hand, that made all the earth drunken; the nations have drunken of her wine; therefore the nations are mad (insane)" (Jeremiah 51:7)

"Should you help the ungodly, and love them that hate the LORD: Therefore is wrath upon thee FROM BEFORE THE LORD." (II Chronicles 19:2)

This once Christian nation has an undeniable history of helping the ungodly and the enemies of God. According to Jeremiah wrath is to be expected upon us. The Twin Towers attack should be no surprise.

In summation, I would say something, on the order of the attack on September 11,th was inevitable and is probably only the beginning of more woes to come because of our great national sins.

"Be not deceived, God is not mocked; for whatsoever a man soweth, that shall he also reap." (Galatians 6:7)

Book Order Form

Quantity	Book Title	Amt	Qty	Total
1 to 11	**Without Controversy** - Pastor Rick Strawcutter	$9.95		
Group Special 12 books	**Without Controversy** - Pastor Rick Strawcutter	$75 postage incl.		
		Order Sub Total		
	(Shipping included when ordering Group Special) - Shipping + 15%			
	Total Contribution			

Order 12 books as a group and shipping is
included. A great way to distribute to
friends or family!

Name: _____

Address: _____

City: _____ State / Zip: _____

Day (___) _____ Eve: (___) _____

E-Mail: _____

Card # _____

Exp. Date: _____ Visa ☐ MC ☐

Name on card: _____

Signature Req: _____

Mail to:

The Church of the Lord Jesus Christ - Dept. TI

P.O. Box 339

Adrian, MI 49221

You may also call in your order at:

Toll Free **1-888-820-2126** or locally in Adrian, MI **(517)-263-1078**

God Bless You, Pastor Rick Strawcutter

www.thechurchinadrian.com

Proclaim Liberty Ministry   www.proclaimliberty.com

Video Order Form

Video #	Name of Video	Amt	Qty	Total
T 972	**Ambassador of a Foreign Government** - Strange things to our ears - Acts 17	$9.95		
T 984	**Buried With Christ in Baptism** Sunday Morning Service with Pastor Strawcutter	$9.95		
T 802	**God's Marriage and Re-marriage to Israel** Sunday Morning Service with Pastor Strawcutter	$9.95		
T 831	**Old Testament 101** Covers the entire Old Testament in a thorough overview in only 60 minutes. **Hailed as the best presentation of Bible basics ever**	$9.95		
T 800	**Interview with Kay Griggs** Pastor Strawcutter's exclusive interview with the wife of Col. George Griggs. She exposes the underworld of military intelligence assassinations, Oswald, McVey and the homosexual connection.	$19.95		
T 979	**World Trade Center - the Real Deal** 9/11 attack with exclusive interviews - Sherman Skolnic and Michael Collins Piper. Includes the Lewinski and Chandra Levy connections.	$19.95		
T 965	**"Pencil Points"** Sunday Morning Service with Pastor Strawcutter	$9.95		
T 986	**In the Last Days Perilous Times Shall Come** Sunday Morning Service just after 9/11 with Pastor Strawcutter	$9.95		
T 968	**We are all Sinners, Called to Repentance** Sunday Morning Service with Pastor Strawcutter	$9.95		
T 969	**The Way It Is** Sunday Morning Service with Pastor Strawcutter	$9.95		
T 875	**"I know He's Alive, I just Saw Him."** Passover Sunday Morning Service with Pastor Strawcutter	$9.95		
T 367	**"Media Terrorism and Mind Control"** This is the famous tape mentioned on page 124. Thousand distributed nationwide	$9.95		

Order 3 or more tapes and the amount is lowered to $9.00 per tape. - excluding T 979 & T 800

Order Sub Total	
Shipping + 15%	
Total Contribution	

Name: _____

Address: _____

City: _____ State / Zip: _____

Day ( ) _____ Eve: ( ) _____

E-Mail: _____

Card # _____

Exp. Date: _____ Visa ☐ MC ☐

Name on card: _____

Signature Req: _____

Mail to: The Church of the Lord Jesus Christ - Dept. TI

P.O. Box 339

Adrian, MI 49221

You may also call in your order at:

Toll Free **1-888-820-2126** or locally in Adrian, MI **(517)-263-1078**

God Bless You, Pastor Rick Strawcutter

www.thechurchinadrian.com